I always believe that your compassion and goodwill
to one another will be a significant factor in creating a unifying
force in any group and also in the country.·

HM King Bhumibol Adulyadej
Kingdom of Thailand

One Anothering Volume 2
A Biblical Guide to A Better Christian Interpersonal Relations
By Marvin A. Marcelino
2021 All Rights Reserved.

Cover Design by Marvin Marcelino

Image credits to:
http://weheartit.com/zizeh/collections/92340177-cute-funny-weird-finger-face
https://www.pinterest.com/pin/325807354271532553/
https://www.buzzfeed.com/mathewguiver/finger-faces-rock
https://www.pinterest.com/creativityarte/art-finger/

Scriptures are from
The Holy Bible: King James Version, copyright 1611 used by permission of
Collins World.
The Holy Bible: Revised Standard Version copyright 1901 by American Bible
Society. Used by permission.
The Holy Bible New International Version, Copyright 1984 by International
Bible Society. Used by permission.

ISBN:
Hardbound:
Mobile/Kindle:
Softbound/Paperback:

Published by;
Poetry Planet Book Publishing House
688 Rosario Pozorrubio, Pangasinan 2435 Philippines
Contact Number: 09554960044
Email: maritesritumalta@gmail.com

One Anothering

A Biblical Guide to A Better
Christian Interpersonal Relations

VOLUME TWO

MARVIN A. MARCELINO

"Never underestimate the infinite love within you
It has the power to transform lives"
MIMI NOVIC

DEDICATED TO
Joshua Marvin my First-born
Mayumi Jasmine the Apple-of-my-eye

Mark Jiro the Seed of Love
Jasmin, my wife, and Inspiration

Acknowledgement

Again thank you for inspiring me to extend this group study activity, I am so inspired to finish writing *this second volume of One Anothering.*

To the many people, thank you for the support and encouragement.

To the young people of that small church in Puting-kahoy Silang, Cavite, who listened to my lecture about conflict resolution one Sabbath afternoon. That small lecture grew into this full-grown book.

To all people who contributed through their unconscious slips-up which are noteworthy for a study.

To the many lovely people who gave several suggestions and improvements to the manuscript.

Thanks to all my friends who gave me a tap on my shoulder and believed in this work.

Jasmin my wife also serves as my *'love-technical-supervisor.'* My three children: Joshua, Mayumi, and Jiro, they serve as my *assistants,* for revealing the fruits of love and labor.

I thank God the most for loving me no matter what I am and for His help in dealing with my being unloving, which have plagued my life. I am truly grateful to God for the love I found in Him.

Marvin Marcelino
Thailand

Perhaps they were right in putting love into books...
Perhaps it could not live anywhere else.

WILLIAM FAULKNER

The fact that we all need and crave for love,
and so little of it could be seen around.

LEO BUSCAGLIA

Preface

THe first book has produced love to some who have read and applied the principles. And to some may take time to grow but I am hopeful that the seed of love will grow in their lives and bear the fruits of love. People crave for love it so happen that it became a rare commodity. Now a days to find love it is like taking a dive into the ocean for a pearl and find it yourself.

People need help and if we take learning from our mistakes that path will take love a long way. For everyone to learn or experience. So, we need to learn and teach people as fast and as many as we can.

This second volume has similar design for personal growth, devotional, and small group activities for interpersonal relations.

This is excellent for home, school, church, and the workplaces. It is a *guidebook, devotional book, activity book*, a *reference book, a Values class textbook, family book; all rolled into one.*

The goal is the same to be able to have a better intrapersonal and interpersonal social relation with another person. We have the same down to earth approach and looking forward that the result be as what Virgil, the philosopher once said.

Nunc scio quit sit amor (Latin)
Now I know what love is

Where there is love there is life
MAHATMA **G**ANDHI

Love is life. And if you miss love, you miss life.
LEO **B**USCAGLIA

How to use this book

There are two ways to use this book.

For Personal Use
Use it as a devotional book.

> The Activity part has questions that are too personal to be made public. You can keep it or share at your disposal.

For Group Use
Follow these six steps if you will be using this book for group study.

Step one. As an opener, do the *Confront* section as instructed, best if each participant own a copy of this book to answer.

Step two. Proceed to the *Confer. Guide Questions for Discussion.* This will serve as an ice breaker for group dynamics. This is best when a facilitator guides the discussions. Try to come up with different views and deal with the pros and cons of the topic at hand.

Step three. Read the *Consider* section loud to the group to gain some insights. You can expand, yet do not go away from the essence.

Step four. Commit section, share tips on how to: This is best if each participant has a Bible to read and to mark.

Step five. Do the Prayer individually or by groups (twos, three or more), especially pray with people whom you are in conflict. The prayer is an avenue to clear out individual differences.

Step six. Let everybody recite the Affirmation part aloud.

Affirmation statements will help you wrap up the discussion by summarizing the principles learned and pledge to keep it.

I do hope you enjoy **One Anothering!**

Contents

Sin will be rampant everywhere
and will cool the love of many.
BOOK OF MATTHEW

The very best credential we can carry
is loving one another.
ELLEN G. WHITE

Introduction

ere it is One Anothering Volume Two! Thank you for the positive responses and requests to add some more topics on how to relate with another person according to the Word of God.

There are a lot of exciting and interesting topics in this volume, go through it and learn more about this love and know how to apply to any one in any means.

Our objective is the same and that is to rediscover the practicality of loving one another; a godly love in action. Let us rediscover the 'how to' of loving others according to the Holy Bible. What do we live for is not to make life difficult for each other? We have come to this world not to be loved, but to love, not to get but to give and not to be served but to serve.

We need to learn all possible ways how truly we love others. That is the reason for having this volume two with similar two basic questions. First, what does it really mean to love one another? Second, how can one really love one another? In the process, we will use the Bible to tell us how to relate with other people.

Why is love becoming a rare commodity now a days? Christ Jesus has said, "Iniquities shall abound and the love of many shall be wax cold." (Matthew 24:12) The prophecy posed as a seemingly insoluble future problem. Christ had already given the solution to the problem of chaos, of conflicts and of misunderstandings. Jesus did not only say that we should love one another, but He demonstrated how to love another.

Good social relation is a way to peace and unity but unforgiving spirit, hate, bitterness is like virus that we get used to and prefer to live with; thus, making this the norm of the century. This is the virus that media love to broadcast, filmmakers love to portray in films. Our senses are sensitized by flooding of these hate spirits.

A famous writer Ellen G. White set the alarm that, "the need of union with Christ and with one another is our only safety in these last days. Let us not make it possible for Satan to point to our church members saying, "Behold how these people standing under the banner of Christ hate one another?"1

"As long as we are in the world we must link with one another. Humanity is interlaced and interwoven with humanity, as Christians we are members one of another. The Lord has made us thus, and when disappointments come, we are not to think worse of one another. We are individual members of a whole body. In helplessness and disappointments, we are fighting the battle of life. Moreover, God has designed us as His sons and daughters, whom He calls His friends to help one another. This is to be part of our practical Christian work."2

We are living in the era where individualism has matured. We are living as people afflicted with the 'kanya-kanya (to each his own) syndrome' and we are all infected. Only the Great Healer can remove a contagious disease from our body, a disease that is never designed and accepted in the place He is preparing for us (John 14:1-3).

As Ellen White confirmed, "Only love can love be awakened." Ralph Waldo Emerson adds, "All mankind loves a lover."

Grace Goudhue Coolidge averred, "Love was not given to the human heart for careless dealings; its spark was given that man might know the divine revealing." "Take heed lest ye forget and be over task by the cares of this present world." (Luke 21:34) "Love is indeed heaven upon the earth," preached William Penn, "since heaven above would not be heaven without it."

Petrach taught, "Love is the crowning grace of humanity, the holiest right of the soul, the golden links which binds us to duty and truth, the redeeming principle that chiefly reconciles the heart of life and in prophetic of eternal good." Benjamin Disraeli agrees, "We are all born for love; it is the principle of existence and its only end." Like Paul's vision "If it be possible as much lives in you, live peaceably with all men."(Roman 12:18)

Marvin Marcelino

If you have knowledge and wisdom
let others light their candle from it.

MARGARET FULLER

They did not teach me how to love,

they showed me how to love.

LEO BUSCAGLIA

Exhort One Another

RECTOR CORRECTOR

Check three from each column.

To exhort others.
☆ ☆ I am not worthy
☆ ☆ I can say it, but I cannot do it
person to do it.
☆ ☆ I think it is none sense
☆ ☆ I just do not care
☆ ☆ I need a seminar
☆ ☆ I need direction

For others to exhort me.
☆ ☆ I cannot give up my pride.
☆ ☆ I need a trusted
☆ ☆ I need ear plugs.
☆ ☆ I will run away.
☆ ☆ Something I need help on
☆ ☆ Is nobody's business.

Give your reasons for each response.

____
____
____

____
____
____

CONFER. Guide questions for discussion

1. What reason/s is one held accountable to another?

2. How can we be accountable to another who is wandering in sin?

3. What rights have one to check another?

4. How should we check another who is committing sin? Give ways.

5. How should one take an exhortation from another? What spirit should one have when being rebuked?

Marvin Marcelino

Exhort One Another

*But exhort one another as long as
it is called today. Hebrews 3:13 RSV*

A boy was misbehaving in class, and the teacher sent him to the principal's office. After hearing the story, he took out a blank folder and wrote the boy's name on the cover. While he was writing, he said to the lad, ʻYou have not been sent to me before. Now I do not know; you might be a good boy, for all I know. Good boys sometimes make mistakes. Now inside on the first page I am making a note why you were sent. As you see, I am making this memorandum in pencil, and I am not bearing on it very hard. If you are never again sent to me this year, I shall erase this from my book, and no one will ever know anything about it.ʼ[3]

George Herbert, an English clergyman preached, ʻIf any speak ill of you fly home to your conscience and examine your heart. If you are guilty, it is just a correction; if not, it is a fair instruction.ʼ At times, we need correcting. We have the strong tendency to believe that what we do is always right, and when someone corrects our misdeeds, we feel bad if not angry.

To exhort is to love. To exhort means to urge to good work, to persuade, to spur, to plead, to prompt, to entreat, to press, or to caution. There are hundreds of definitions but the essence of this is to correct others so they will do what is right.ʼ

A famous writer said, ʻAll who would advocate the principles of truth need to receive the heavenly oil of love, under all circumstances reproof should be spoken in love.ʼ[4] Exhort with great patience and instruction ʻ2Timothy 4:2ʼ We must correct one another with all the patience and endurance until the person does it right, correcting gently that they may repent ʻ2Timothy 2:25ʼ

We must correct constructively one another's error so the erring will positively accept his error and change for good. Exhort with all the truth (Titus 5:15) We correct by exposing the wrong, extract the truth and exacting the right, therefore; we should exhort with all suffering (patience) (2Timothy 4:2)

If it takes time, treasures, or even years to correct one another, don' give up. Exhort with many words, which means do a lot of explaining. Exhort to strengthen one another to be sober minded (to be serious about spiritual matters) (Titus 2:6) We must correct another until he will come to his senses and think it seriously, exhort one another to obedience (Titus 2:9) We need to correct one another to be obedient to God. Exhort to continue in faith (Acts 14:22) We must correct continually the unfaithful and encourage the faithless.

It is hardest to correct people who continuously deny their glaring error. D. L Moody is right when he illustrated, ·The best way to show that a stick is crooked is not to argue about it, or to spend time denouncing it, but by laying a straight stick alongside it.·

·Though their hearts may be as hard as a beaten highway while logic may fail to move, arguments are powerless and apparently it may be useless effort to present the Savior to them. Christs love revealed in personal ministry, may have suffered just to win the stony heart.[5]

Exhort one another to receive him Christ Jesus (Acts 18:27) We must correct one's doubts about our Savior Jesus Christ. Exhort to provoke unto love and to good works until you see hope approaching (Hebrews 10:24)   Allow the teachings and love of Christ to moisten the hard soil of the heart for the blessing of humanity.

Exhorting is one expression of love and a responsibility that needs to be exercised. Let expression of sympathy and love which will not blister our tongue flow from your lips. Let others feel the warmth which love, can create in the heart, and educate the professed Disciples of Christ, to correct the evil that have so long existed. Selfishness, coldness and hardheartedness all these traits reveal the fact that Christ is not abiding in the soul.[6]

Divine love made its most touching appeals when it called upon us to manifest the same tender compassion that Christ manifested. Those men who are unselfish toward their brothers have true love for God. The true Christian will not willingly permit the soul in peril and need to go unwarned, uncared for.[7]

Have you been correcting one another?

HOW TO EXHORT ONE ANOTHER

- ❑ Remember that you are a royal priest (1Peter 2:9)
- ❑ Be firm but gentle and loving.
- ❑ Be constructive and creative in correcting another.
- ❑ Talk to the person privately or with a witness. Tell the person the consequences of a particular wrong action.
- ❑ Restore the person gently who is caught in sin (Gal. 6:1)
- ❑ Keep guarded in truth (1 John 4:20)
- ❑ Remember God is correcting our ways (Hebrews 12:7)
- ❑ Harden not your heart (Hebrews 3:8-12)
- ❑ Exhort more often (Acts 15:32), and patiently (2Tim. 4:2)
- ❑ Rebuke sharply but gently (Titus 1:13)
- ❑ Focus on the behavior not on the person.
- ❑ Speak the truth in the spirit of love (Ephesians 4:15)
- ❑ Check how you say it. Criticize constructively.
- ❑ Go direct to the person, no sidelines, no proxy.
- ❑ Earn your right to constructive criticism (Matthew 7:4, 5)
- ❑ Use helpful and kind words (Ephesians 4:29)
- ❑ Remember that corrections are the way of Life. (Prov. 6:23)
- ❑

PRAYER

Dear Heavenly Father, I confess that often I ignore to correct the errors of ____________. Help me Father to have the courage to stand against someone's wrongdoing. I beg the Holy Spirit to direct my way in correcting those who are committing sin. This I pray in the name of Jesus Christ my Lord Savior. Amen.

AFFIRMATION

I am to uphold righteousness and I am to call sin by its right name. I am to be firm as the needle to the pole. I will stand without fear and favor for the right and just.

Marvin Marcelino

We are each of us angels with only one wing,
and we can only fly embracing each other.

LUCIANO DE CRESCENZO

Do your duty and leave the rest to heaven.

PIERRE CORNEILLI

Carry One Another's Burden

BURDEN CARRIER

Write down names of burdened persons, whom you have helped or plan to help.

1. Yesterday   Today   Tomorrow

__________   __________ --   __________
__________   __________   __________

2. How you can help carry others burdens?

__________   __________ --   __________
__________   __________   __________

3. What blessings have you received while helping others?

____

CONFER. Guide questions for discussion

1. What motivation should we have for carrying one another's burdens?

2. Why are consoling words·not enough to carry one another's burden?

3. How can a Christian carry his own burden while carrying another's burden at the same time?

4. Can you give an actual example of a person who, amid having his own heavy burden, found time and strength to carry another's burden?

5. How can you convince a person to help others even if he feels that he is less fortunate than the people around him?

Marvin Marcelino

Carry One Another's Burden

Bear one another's burdens,   Galatians 6:2 RSV

Two brothers worked together on a family farm. One was single, and the other is married with children. They equally shared what they grew and produced. However, one day the single brother said to himself, It is not right that I should receive an equal share of our produce, and profit. After all, I am alone, and my needs are simple, but my poor brother has a wife and children. In the middle of the night, he took a sack of grain from the bin, crept over the field between their houses, and dumped the grain into his brother's bin.

Meanwhile, unknown to him, his brother had the same thought. He said to himself. It is not right that we should share the produce and profit equally. After all, I am married, and I have a wife to look after me and my children for years to come. He too in the middle of the night took a sack of grain from his bin and sneaking across the field, to deposit it into his brother's bin.

For years, both were puzzled as to why their supply did not dwindle. Well, one night it just happened that they both left their houses at the same time. In the dark, they bumped into each other carrying their sacks. Each was startled, but then it dawned on them what was happening. They dropped their sacks and embraced one another. Suddenly, the dark sky lit up, and a voice from heaven spoke, Here, at last, is the place where I will build my temple. For where brothers meet in love, there my presence shall dwell.[8]

It does no good to offer consoling words to a man in distress; his real friend is a friend indeed when deeds are needed. That is as true today as when Plautos uttered that in

2003 BC., Publius Syrius in 43 BC, wrote a quotation, ʻProsperity begets friends and adversity prove them.·Everyone has his own share of private or corporate problems. Not one is exempted from the everyday load of burden.

Paul advised us to help despite our heavy load. We must help others along the way. Regardless of how heavy the loads we are carrying, we still can lend our other hand to help others. Acknowledging another's burden is indeed a noble act, but the Scriptures require us to go an extra mile from just learning what the ones burden is. It is telling us to carry the burden as well. Yes, carry one another's burden on top of your burden. One needs someone to help him carry his burden.

What I appreciate about my fellow Filipinos are their resiliency and endurance. They fight to the last strength, to the last breath, and it is not until they have exhausted all effort that they admit they need a helping hand. However, we do not have to wait for them to ask. Let us meet them where they are.

Cicero tells of carrying anothers burden. He said, ·To bear each others burdens, never to ask for anything inconsistent with virtue and rectitude, and not only serve and love but also respect each other.· While Charles Dudley tells of the reward, he said, ·It is one of the beautiful compensations of this life that no one can sincerely try to help another without helping himself.·

There is a Persian proverb that says, ·What I kept, I lost; what I spent, I had; what I gave, I have.· Let me modify it this way, ·When I ignored anothers burden, mine was heavy. When I carried anothers burden, mine was lighter. When we both carried each others burden, we both felt relieved.·

Have you been carrying one anothers burden?

HOW TO CARRY ONE ANOTHER'S BURDEN

- ❏ Pity the poor, because in doing so you lend to the Lord (Proverbs 19:17).
- ❏ Endure hardship like a good soldier of Christ (2Timothy 3:2).
- ❏ Be openhanded toward your brother and toward the poor and needy in your land (Deuteronomy 15:11).
- ❏ Do not be self-seeking (1Corinthians 13:5).
- ❏ Have mercy on your fellow servant (Matthew 18:33).
- ❏ Do not be hard-hearted, or tight-fisted towards another (Deuteronomy. 15:7).
- ❏ Help those who are truly in need (1Timothy 5:9-16).
- ❏ Be kind; it is one of the characteristics of love (1Corinthians 13:4).
- ❏ In your abundance, supply the wants of others (2Corinthians 8:13, 14).
- ❏ Find grace and help in times of need (Hebrews 4:16).
- ❏ Help others, so when they will be there for you when you need help (Ecclesiastes 4:10).

PRAYER

Dear Heavenly Father, I admit that oftentimes I neglect to carry ___________'s burdens, which I should be doing despite my personal burdens. Help me, Father, to carry anothers burdens the way Jesus did. I beg the Holy Spirit to help me comfort those who are heavily laden. This I pray in the name of Jesus Christ, my Lord Savior. Amen.

AFFIRMATION

I am to carry the burdens of other people despite my heavy personal burdens. Only by doing so can I let other people know about God's love.

Confession implies that we are
assuming responsibilities for our actions.

CHARLES STANLEY

Confession is not a sign of weakness
but of maturity and courage.

AUTHOR UNKNOWN

Confess Your Sin To One Another

CONFESSOR'S COMPRESSOR

1. Do this in front of a mirror. Imagine that the person in the mirror is the offended party. Look at the image straight in the eye, and say this.

I did not intend to hurt you with my jokes, and I was insensitive. I am terribly sorry. Please forgive me.

You can replace the wordings of the sentence. Experiment on different voices (high pitch, low, harsh, soft,) you will know the difference.

2. People whom I have offended and need to confess to.

___________   ___________ ___________

3. Of all the wrongs I have done to others this I will not confess.

____

CONFER. Guide questions for discussion

1. Why do we have a hard time confessing our sins to someone we have hurt?

2. In what spirit should an offender have when confessing?

3. Have you heard a false confession? How did you deal with it?

4. How should we treat a person who offended us and wants to reconcile with us?

5. Should confessions of the offender be made public? What would you do if the confession is a sensitive issue?

6. Why should we confess so soon?

Confess Your Sin To One Another

Therefore, confess your sin to one another.
James 5:16 RSV

Mahatma Gandhi told the following experience. 'When I was fifteen years old, I stole something because I was in debt. I stole a golden bracelet that belonged to my father, but I could not stand the burden of my guilt. So, I went to him, but as I stood, I was so ashamed that I could not open my mouth. I wrote down my confession on a piece of paper. As I handed it to him, my whole body trembled. My father read the note, closed his eyes, and tore it to pieces. All he said was, 'Think nothing of it.' Then he took me in his arms and from that moment on, I began to love my father more than I had ever done before.'

To love is to confess to one another. *Exomolegeu* is a Greek word, which means to acknowledge, or to admit. Confessing is hard, especially when we are not used to it; we find it to be the hardest thing to do. Admitting one's fault to another is not a joke. We think it is better to save one's face than be exposed to shame.

Let us take Adam, Eve, and the serpent's insincerity in their confessions. They were trying to avoid by passing their guilt to another - Adam to God for giving him Eve as a wife, and Eve to the serpent (Genesis 3:12-13). Cain, instead of admitting his error, also complained against God's injustice (Genesis 4:1-16).

When there is a sin committed before two parties, gaps are created. A wound is made because of a mere mistake. Did you know that it is only through confessing that healing comes? Jonah did that when he confessed that he was the reason for the storm that affected other people in the ship,

Marvin Marcelino

and everything went well. (Jonah 1:4-16)

Ellen White, in her book *Christ's Object Lessons*, said, "If we have in any way grieved or wounded others, it is our duty to confess our fault and seek reconciliation. This is an essential preparation for us to come before God in faith to ask His blessings. When the Holy Spirit moves in the human minds, all petty complaints and accusation of this man and his fellowman will be put away. The bright beam of the Sun of Righteousness will shine into the chambers of mind and heart... There all pride, all accusations, all self-deceptions will forever have an end."[9]

Repentance without amendment is like continually pumping air into a leaking tire without mending the leak. Thomas Fuller counseled, "One cannot repent too soon because one does not know how soon it may be too late." Let us not be deceived. It is okay to be cheerful, but if our cheerfulness hurts or disregards others' rights because of our foolish jokes, trifling words, sarcastic remarks, and condemnation, when the inclination is so strong, let us take note that we become insensitive to another's feelings.

I like Charles Stanley's brief explanation. "Confession implies that we are assuming responsibilities for our actions. All who endeavor to excuse or conceal their sins and permit them to remain upon the books of heaven, unconfessed and unforgiven will be overcome by Satan."[10]

So, always check oneself if you have hurt someone. It is in self check that we can avoid gaps. The scripture says, "Do not let the sun set without having reconciliation." The reason is not so popular – that when an unforgiving offense has gone overnight, the hurt seed goes deep into the subconscious mind where it will germinate. There, it springs and is occasionally visited and nourished by resentment. It blooms into hatred. It is cherished, cultivated, and eventually matures to a full-grown crime.

When one confesses, do it personal and private, and in the

presence of a witness (Matthew 5:21-24). Admitting an error is not a personality of weakness, but a sign of one's strength. It is not enough to say, 'I'm sorry' for it may not cover the damage sin had made but love may cover it all. Love rejoices not in iniquity, but rejoice in the truth…when sins are confessed, and wrongs are corrected…·[11]

Go and confess your sin to one another.

HOW TO CONFESS SIN TO ONE ANOTHER

- ❏ Be openhearted and transparent.
- ❏ Read Matthew 5:21-24 for guidelines.

>First, go to the offended person-ALONE.

>If you fail, go back with a witness.

>If witnesses fail, bring it to the council.

- ❏ Confess in the presence of many (1Timothy 6:12)
- ❏ Confess to the Lord (Psalm 32:5)
- ❏ Do not cherish sin in your heart, otherwise the Lord will not hear you (Psalms 66:18)
- ❏ Do not let sin rule over you (Psalms 119:133)
- ❏ Invite the Holy Spirit to accompany you to the offended party.
- ❏ Use soft words (Proverbs 15:1)
- ❏ Accept the truth even if it hurts.
- ❏ Whatsoever is true, honest, just, pure lovely, and of good report...think of these (Philippians 4:8)
- ❏ Confess to obtain mercy (Proverbs 28:13)

PRAYER

Dear Heavenly Father, I admit that I have not confessed my sin against ___________. Help me, Father, to have the courage to confess this sin that I have been keeping in my heart for quite a long time. I beg the Holy Spirit to guide my heart that I may find peace and reconciliation. This I pray in the name of Jesus Christ my Lord and Savior. Amen.

AFFIRMATION

I am to confess to people I have hurt. In confessing and admitting my wrong, I am made strong for I am a child of the God of reconciliation.

He prayeth well who loveth well.
He prayeth best who loveth best.
SAMUEL TAYLOR COLERIDGE

As we attempt to live like Christ,
in action, words, and deeds,
We'll follow His design for prayers
and pray for others' need.
J. DAVID BRANON

Pray For One Another

CONFRONT.

PRAYER PAYER
Write names of people who...

I will pray for.   I have prayed for.

_______________   _______________
_______________   _______________

I wish would have prayed for me.   .

_______________   _______________
_______________   _______________

2. For me to pray effectively for others I need...

____

CONFER. _Guide questions for discussion_

1. Why do we need to pray for one another?

2. Have you experienced praying for one another? How did you feel?

3. Have you experienced someone praying for you? How did you feel after the prayer?

4. What positive suggestions have you discovered in this section that helped revive your prayer life?

5. Do you have a prayer burden list? (Have one.)

6. What do you think would hinder one from praying for somebody?

Pray For One Another

Pray for one another. James 5:16 RSV

Two little boys had argued all day as only two brothers can. Their dad scolded the older lad, but he defended himself by saying, 'But John was rude to me.' That night, the three of them knelt at their bedside for their bedtime prayers. After the two had finished, the elder son kept on praying softly. The father asked him what he had told God in that extra prayer. He answered, 'I asked Him to make Johnny a better boy.'[12]

Prayer is the ultimate arbitrator of all differences, the best promoter of true friendships, and the best cure for envy and jealousy. Are there people who dislike or shun you? Pray for them and you will be more patient and charitable. One has made another happy and at peace living in a chaotic world due to a shared prayerful life.

There is truth in the words of Robert McCracken, 'Prayer for others not only transforms the dispositions, and it energizes the will. It helps our imagination to picture the situation of other human beings; it troubles the conscience and kindles the affection in the heart. Finally, it moves the will to action.'

No person in his right mind will ever say 'no' to an offered prayer. Even a stranger you catch along the way cannot refuse. He will be amazed and thankful. One thing is certain, you have made him feel very good! Prayer is dynamic! Use it and you will discover you cannot stop short of prayer. You may never know that beneath the human skin are needs that need addressed, questions answered, burdens removed, and depression uplifted; through prayers.

Never underestimate the power of prayer! With your generous offering and intercession, you can never tell the benefits of your prayer. ·Prayer,· alludes Jean Calvin, ·..brings us into the deepest and highest work of the human spirit.· Charles and Virginia Sell, in their book *Spiritual Intimacy for Couples,* said, ·Prayer awakens us to recognize all we desire and the need to come to God.·

We pray together to invite God's presence, for where there are two or three gathered in His name, His presence is in their midst ·Matthew 18:20· Praying with others testifies of an active God when two or more of His children come together. God delights in human activity such as praying for each other.

Why do we need to pray for one another? Praying for together helps express our anxieties. Praying together wipes away indifferences. Praying together enables us to comply with the will of God. It helps us expose the attitude we have for one another. It helps us reach others ·Philippians 1:3·

·Those who bring their petition to God, claiming His promises while they do not comply with the conditions, ·like applying *One Anothering*· insult Jehovah.[13] A little girl was saying her evening prayers. She must have some interesting experiences during the day, for she prayed, ·Lord, make all the people good; and all the good people nice.·

May this prayer by Henry Woodsworth Longfellow be your prayers too, *·Lord, help me live from day to day, in such a*

forgetful way that even when I kneel to pray; my prayers be for others.·

Will you pray for someone now?

HOW TO PRAY FOR ONE ANOTHER

- ❑ Read Matthew 5:21-24 for guidelines.
- ❑ Read John 17 and learn how Jesus prays for others.
- ❑ Pray for power in this manner (Colossian 1:11).
- ❑ Pray for productivity of others' lives (Colossians 1:10).
- ❑ Strive together in prayers (Romans 15:30).
- ❑ Pray that others would know God's will. (1John 5:14, 15).
- ❑ Pray that you will do God's will.
- ❑ Have a prayer burden list.
- ❑ You can pray through the phone.
- ❑ Be specific with your prayer.
- ❑ Ask the person about his specific need to be addressed through prayer.
- ❑ Pray with joy (Philippians 1:4).
- ❑ Get a copy of the book *The Next Level Prayer* book.

PRAYER

Dear Heavenly Father, I confess that I often neglect to pray for ___________. Teach me Father the way Jesus prayed. I beg the Holy Spirit to intercede for me and give me words to pray. I pray this in the name of Jesus Christ, my Lord and Savior. Amen.

AFFIRMATION

I am a prayerful, spirit-filled person of God. I will always pray for others as Jesus prayed for me before the Father. I will pray for others that they, too, might find peace and blessings from God.

Marvin Marcelino

Washing another's dirty feet,
is like washing one's heart of sin.
MARVIN MARCELINO

Feet washing is a work of sealing
the reconciliation processes.
ELLEN G. WHITE

Wash One Another's Feet

FEET WASHER

1. Supply names that have something to do with your feet washing activity.

Who have washed my feet; _______________________________

Whose feet I have washed; _______________________________

Who I wish will wash my feet; _______________________________

Whose feet I will never wash; _______________________________

2. How do you feel every time you do the feet washing activity with another person?

____

CONFER. *Guide questions for discussion*

1. What is the real essence of foot washing? Explain.

2. Why would someone not dare to wash another's feet?

3. How does the washing of feet bring about reconciliation?

4. Should one be choosy in washing another's feet?

5. What is the role of humility in feet washing?

Marvin Marcelino

Wash One Another's Feet

You also ought to wash one another's feet. John 13:14 RSV

A certain tribe in Kenya is called Masai. Most of the Masai were cattle raisers. They roam from one place to another with their herds. Whenever a priest visits them on his pastoral rounds, he will pitch a tent a few meters away from their pastures. He then collects a basketful of green grass and brings it to the tribe settlement. Green grass among the desert-dwelling people was a sign of love. The basket of green grass passed from one family to another. However, if one family were not living in peace with others, the basket is not allowed to pass. The priest waits, if the basket is delayed, he knows that the tribal peace is disturbed. Nevertheless, seldom the basket is delayed. Normally, families accept the basket and try to keep it green and moving, so they patch up their differences in a hurry and restore peace.·[14]

Washing is good. It gives you a good and a refreshing feeling. I want you to go back to the scene of John 13, verses 1 to 13. Jesus stood up from the supper table and tied a towel on his waist. Then he poured water in the basin and began to wash the disciples' feet. Jesus approached Peter. Peter asked, ·Are you going to wash my feet Lord?· The Lord replied, ·You may not understand now, but you will realize later.· ·No, Stop,· Peter, insisted, ·I won't let you wash my feet.· The Lord said, ·If you will not let me wash your feet, you have no part in me.· With philosophical thought, Peter replied, ·Okay, wash not only my feet include my whole body.·

The essence of washing feet reveals that this is directly telling the person ·I have no bad intention or motive against you brother. My mind and conscience are clear I have totally forgotten all my unpleasant and negative thoughts I had against you. I only pray that you may have more blessings to come. I am now washing your feet with all humility, placing down all my pride, all my status because I want you brother to be a part of me. Jesus bids us to do the same, If you call me Lord, then do the example I did (John 13:15) If you are for Jesus trash your pride; we are servants, we are messengers, and we are no greater than the Master.

Ray Pritchard in his book *Man of Honor* shared, In the olden days, 1) Feet washing was considered an ordinary sign. 2) It is by definition smelly and humiliating. 3) It will never go out of style because you never run out of feet to wash. Ellen White gave a deeper insight, Feet washing is as the work of sealing the reconciliation process. As Christ celebrated the ordinance with His disciples, conviction came to the heart of all to save Judas. So we shall be convicted as Christ speaks to our hearts. The fountain of the soul will be broken. The mood will be energized, springing with activity and life, will break down every barrier that has caused dissension and alienation.[15]

During the feet washing ceremony, do not try to avoid washing the feet of the person you have a grudge with. It does not help your soul, neither your health. An adage goes like this, He who cannot forgive others breaks the bridge over which he must pass himself. For a grudge does not get better when nursed, rather it turns into hatred and bitterness.

The Lord bids us to love our enemies (Luke 6:27) Forgive and forget; forgiveness helps your soul and forgetting helps your body. Feet washing is each ones responsibility; as ministers of reconciliation (2Corinthians 5:15, 18) Go wash as many feet as you can for by doing so, you are building up peace and reconciliation with another.

Thank Christ Jesus for instituting the feet washing ceremony during the communion service. It is indeed a down-to-earth practice of reconciliation between two individuals and between God and man.

Have you been washing each others feet?

Marvin Marcelino

HOW TO WASH ONE ANOTHER'S FEET

- ❏ Ask God for a clean, new heart (Psalm 51:10).
- ❏ ·Wash· yourself first.
- ❏ ·Wash· your heart from selfish motive.
- ❏ ·Wash· your heart from pride, bad intentions, hurts, and revenge.
- ❏ Say sorry and explain why you have done such to the offended party.
- ❏ Remember you are a Minister of Reconciliation (2Corinthians 5:15).
- ❏ Remember you are Christ's Ambassador (2Corinthians 5:20).
- ❏ Bear in mind God will judge every secret thing of man by Christ Jesus (Romans 2:16).
- ❏ Make yourself part of others by feet washing (John 13:8).

PRAYER

Dear Heavenly Father, I confess that I passed up the opportunity to wash __________'s feet. Remind me Father of the humility that Jesus has demonstrated when He washed the disciples' feet. I beg the Holy Spirit to give me a humble heart that I may wash the feet of those whom I am to reconcile with. This I pray in the name of Jesus Christ, my Lord. Amen.

AFFIRMATION

I am a peacemaker. By washing anothers feet I am showing humility. Through this, I will be able to help build reconciliation with one another and make peace a reality.

The first duty of love is to listen.
PAUL TILLICH

Let us be Christ's true disciple,
looking to anothers needs.

Making stormy pathway smooth,
by gentle words or deeds.

THORSON

Marvin Marcelino

Comfort One Another

CONSOLE CASSEROLE

1. Rank your talent comforting another, 1 being the highest and 6 being the least

___Giving comfort to the bereaved.

___Giving comfort to the victim of great loss.

___Giving comfort to the terminally ill.

___Giving comfort to depressed and anxious.

___Giving comfort to the poor.

___Giving comfort to the needy.

2. Rate your spiritual talent in comforting another.

Poor 1 2 3 4 5 6 7 8 9 10 Best

CONFER. *Guide questions for discussion*

1. What motivates one to have the initiative to comfort another?

2. What will hinder one to comfort another?

3. Should giving comfort be rendered only when affliction or tragedy is present?

4. How can we render comfort to another even without affliction?

5. Give reasons why the spiritual gift of giving comfort was given to man.

Comfort One Another

Comfort one another. 1 Thessalonians 4.18 RSV

A little boy who was holding a little sparrow with a broken wing. A kind old woman came along and asked the boy, ·Would you like me to take this sparrow home and nurse it back to health? Promised, I will bring it back to this garden when it has healed and let it fly free again.· The little boy thought for a moment. Then he said, ᛁ will take care of this bird myself· he paused, and added ᛓecause you see I understand this bird.· The old woman could not understand what the boy meant until the little boy stood up and saw his legs in a cast.[16]

Giving comfort is a spiritual talent that everyone can easily practice. The only thing one need for another is concern. Grace Noll Crowell's clearly portrays this in her poem, *One in Sorrow.·*

Let me come in where you are weeping, friend.
And let me take your hand. I have known yours,
I can understand.

Let me come in still beside you in your grief;
I would not bid you to stop your weeping,
Friend, tears bring relief. Let me come in

I have known a sorrow such as yours
and I understand.·

·The first gift of friendship is companionship. The second is the gift of hope. A good friendship affirms that good things can still take that place no matter what the magnitude of loss.· that was from Robert Veringa's book *A Gift of Hope.* Joyce Hugget shares of her experiences in listening to suffering people in her book *Listening to Others.* She wrote, ᛁ have not done anything. I just listened.· She concluded, ·The effective way of helping

Marvin Marcelino

others is through listening.·

Everyone has daily bombardment of cares and burdens in life. That makes us think that we are the only person afflicted with gargantuan problems. These give us thoughts that others does not care about, and we resolve to self-pity. Did you know that one becomes active again when another comes and extend cares with a simple How are you doing?· Relief, comfort and peace come to those who pray for you and to those who share their blessing to comfort another.

A picture of a community helping and comforting one another is a wonderful description of how a Christian should relate with one another. When a member of our community, our church, our family suffers a tragedy, we should come in and help that person until he is back to his feet.

There is a species of bird called the bluebird, which is a perfect example of how one gives comfort and assistance to another. Bluebirds are unique in the sense that when one of the parents of a brood dies, another bluebird will come to help the afflicted family. They have such an instinct to render comfort to other bluebirds. Female bluebirds will assist the widowed in rearing her young. The male bluebirds will help in searching for food. They will do this until the family is ready to stand on their own, what a community!

It is not about the lack of love of the bluebirds. It is all about available neighbors welcome to help just as though it is their appointed task.[17]

The birds have followed certain rules like Julia Fletcher Carney's thoughts that say, Little deeds of kindness, little words of love help make the earth happy like the heaven above.·

You will never understand how anothers toothache feels if you do not have one. Have you been comforting one another?

HOW TO COMFORT ONE ANOTHER

- ❏ Giving comfort is good for the soul (Proverbs 11:17).
- ❏ Pray for each other's sorrows.
- ❏ Show care through small kindness.
- ❏ Encourage, keep high each other's hope.
- ❏ Be always ready to give comfort.
- ❏ Give/share a promise from the Bible when one is down.
- ❏ Listen - it's good or the soul (Proverbs 11:17).
- ❏ Share a thoughtful word of hope.
- ❏ Ask God to give you a caring heart.
- ❏ Comfort the feeble minded (1Thessalonians 5:14).
- ❏ Be still. Allow God to do help you (Exodus 14:14).
- ❏ Encouraging and build up others (1Thessalonians 5:13).
- ❏ Listen, do not be selfish (Jeremiah 13:15).
- ❏ Be merciful for God honors those who are merciful. (Proverbs 14:31).
- ❏ Be merciful. God is merciful too (Luke 6:36).

PRAYER

Dear Heavenly Father, I admit that I neglected to comfort ___________. Thank you Father for the Holy Spirit, who comforts me in my sorrows, and to Jesus who showed me how to comfort the afflicted. I beg the Holy Spirit to guide my heart to be sensitive to those who need my comforting presence. This I pray in the name of Jesus Christ, my Lord and Savior, Amen.

AFFIRMATION

God's love to me is overflowing. I am merciful and caring to those who are in need of my comfort.

Mine honor is my life, both grow in one;
Take honor from me; and my life is done.

WILLIAM SHAKESPEARE

True honor and nobility do not reside in blood
but in man's character, formed in the
atmosphere of reason and trained by honest work.

APOLINARIO MABINI

Honor One Another

HONOR KEEPER

Complete the sentence.

1. Giving honor to me means...

____

2. I render honor to another by...

____

____

____

3. My respect toward another dampens when...

____

CONFER. *Guide questions for discussion*

1. What are the reasons why we must honor one another?

2. Can we give due honor to everyone? Defend your answer.

3. Give ways on how you can honor another you think is undesirable.

4. What does 'attitude' have to do with honoring another? Why should attitude must be checked?

Honor One Another

Honor one another. Romans 12:10a RSV

Once there was a lonely man named Thomas. He outlived all his friends, and hardly anyone knew him. He died. A man had a feeling that no one will go to Thomas' funeral, so the man decided to follow him to his last resting place. It was raining hard. At the gate of the cemetery was another man in an army raincoat. The soldier came to the graveside for the ceremony.

When it was over, he gave a salute only fit for a king. He and the soldier walked away, when the wind blew open his raincoat revealed his rank as a brigadier. The Brigadier said, Perhaps you are wondering what I am doing here. Years ago, Thomas was my church Bible teacher; I was a wild lad and a sore trial to him. He never knew what he did for me, but I owe old Thomas what I became, and today I had come to salute him at the end. Thomas earned an honor, though a rank is honorable, but none can surpass the honor a Christian can ever do and give.[18] Give respect to whom respect is due, honor to whom honor is appropriate (Romans 13:7). Loving is giving honor to one another. To honor means to give praise, to esteem, to value, to consider, and to give distinction to another person. To honor is to respect, and respecting is another way to love. Honor applies to all aspects of human activity toward others. We can raise one's respect level by praising the good wherever we find it. Lowell Fillmore is right, If we just keep on honoring the Christian virtues then many will want them.

Honor another's personality; remember his behavior may even be a result of a bad past. The Bible dealt much in this subject. Honor is a due, and one must give to whom it is appropriate. Honor are due to parents (Exodus 10:12), to grandparents (Leviticus 19:32), to one another (John 5:44), to all men and kings (1Peter 2:17), to governments or authorities (Romans 13), to Christ (John 5:23) and to God (Exodus 20:3-6).

One's right to hit other stops where one's nose tip starts. One's right to sing ends when someone's turn to sleep begins. One's right ends where the rights of others start. To honor is to respect. One's attitude towards other reveals one's attitude and belief toward his God. A wrong attitude toward one another is not pleasing to God.

The act of those that discount the value of another is contrary to the nature of God. If you have the spirit of Christ you will love as brethren; you will honor the humble disciple in his house because God loves him as much as He loves you. He recognizes no caste. He places his own signet upon men, not by their rank, not by their wealth, not by intellect or greatness but their oneness with Christ.[19]

One's attitude will tell of how one honor another. Honor them and they will honor you in return for Jesus said, Do unto others what you wish others would do unto you (Matthew 7:12) Honor another even if he does not meet your standard or expectations. Let us read what the Bible says, put others above ourselves (Romans 12:10), ask others opinion (Hebrews 12:14), consider other's response and feelings (James 3:2-5), and think about the consequences of our actions (Galatians 5:22).

In the desire for honor, one must not think about it. Should we hate a person who is hungry of honor? People honor who is worthy of honor. One must earn honor, it is never for a bribe or sale. The one who honors is the one loves. Remember Albert Schweitzer's thoughts, Only those who respect the personality of others can be of real loving to them. Truly, respect is earned respect one another.

Do you honor one another?

HOW TO HONOR ONE ANOTHER

- ❑ Honor to whom honor is due (Romans 13:7)
- ❑ Show respect to everyone (1Peter 2:17)
- ❑ Honor all men (1Peter 2:17)
- ❑ Be careful in exercising your freedom so it does not become a stumbling block to the weak (1Corinthians 8:9)
- ❑ Honor everyone who does well (Romans 2:10)
- ❑ Honor thy father and thy mother(Exodus 20:12)
- ❑ Honor the old people (Leviticus 19:32)
- ❑ Honor the government (Romans 13)
- ❑ Put others above you (Romans 12:10)
- ❑ Ask others opinion too (Hebrews 12:14)
- ❑ Consider other people's feeling (Daniel 7:2-5)
- ❑ Consider good virtues (Galatians 5:22)
- ❑ Honor others if you want to be honored (Matthew 7:12)
- ❑ Honor every person (Galatians 3:27,28)
- ❑ Do not honor the proud and liar (Psalms 90:4)
- ❑ Honor every person (Galatian3:27,28)
- ❑

PRAYER

Dear Heavenly Father, I admit that I do not honor ___________., because I am too ___________. Teach me Father how to honor and respect. Jesus gave me honor by dying for me. I beg the Holy Spirit to direct my heart to render respect and honor to whom it is due. This I pray in the name of Jesus Christ my Lord. Amen.

AFFIRMATION

I am to honor those of my equal, to those below me and, most to those above me. For whosoever I honor, honors me also.

Marvin Marcelino

Let go, why do cling to pain?
Why hold onto the very thing,
which keep you from hope and love?
BHUDDIST PROVERBS

But children, you should never let
such angry passion rise;
Your little hands were never made
to tear each others eyes..

ISAAC WATTS

Do Not Destroy One Another

FACE WRECKER
Have you been involved in the following?

A smear campaign against another (Job 13.4; 30.1)
Yes or No? Explain.

____

Agree with others criticism about another (Job19.2)
Yes or No? Explain.

____

Stand firm to what is true and just (Job 23.11,12)
Yes or No? Explain.

____

Regretted to what you have said or done against another (Job 42.6)
Yes or No? Explain.

____

Prayed for your critics, haters or online bashers (Job 42.8,10)
Yes or No? Explain.

____

CONFER. Guide questions for discussion

1. Why do people resolve to destroy one another?

2. Why is shaming another in public·is compared to the shedding of blood? Explain.

3. How can we overcome the spirit of destroying one another?

Marvin Marcelino

4. How do you deal with a person who destroys another?

5. What could be our best defense from those that destroy us? Defend your answer.

   a. Get even
   b. Pray
   c. Have Christ's character

Do Not Destroy One Another

But if you bite and devour one another...
Galatians 5:15 RSV

Lucy was fired from her work. She had been in the company for a year. Her supervisor does not like her; she was a threat and became a rival for the coming promotion. The newly hired was a niece of the manager. Later Lucy found out that her supervisor befriended the newly hired and conspired to destroy her reputation. The management favored more the rumor than Lucy.

The cynic is one who fails to see good qualities in a person and never fails to see bad ones. He is the human owl, a vigilant in darkness and blind to light, hunting for victims and never stops looking for prey. Henry Ward Beecher wrote, ·The cynic puts all human action in two classes _openly bad and secretly bad.·

Loving one another is not destroying one another. Destroying is not love. To destroy means to annihilate, exterminate, extinguish, quench, eradicate, ruin, obliterate, efface, extirpate, cancel, tear down, demolish, pull down, shatter, devastate or break. Destroying one another is a form of attitude what Filipinos call the '*crab mentality*' that subtly let it loose as time and occasion calls it. However, in fairness to the real crabs, they never have in mind or do such.

The Bible is right, in destroying one another we

are destroying ourselves. To keep lips from slips, four things to observe with care: to whom you speak, of whom you speak, and how and where you speak. The Talmud said, 'Shaming another in public is like shedding blood.' That means it is better for a man to cast himself into a flaming oven than to be shamed in public. 'Anger,' Abraham Husdai said, 'begins with madness and ends in regret.' This is mostly the main reasons for revenge and hate crimes.

'Resentment have ill effects in the mind, body and most of all to the soul,' according to Dr. Jane Stingham. Resentment comes from the Latin word, meaning, 'to feel again.' When we resent, we allow the negative emotions we felt at the time of a hurt, a disappointment, or a betrayal to come back long after the event is over. When we resent we repeatedly keep on flooding our system with poisons. Resentment is cancer to the personality that is as deadly as any serious diseases.

Thus, at times, we are tempted to get even· or payback· but it is not an idea that God approves (Luke 6.27-31) 'The largest share of the annoyance of life is the daily corroding care; its heartaches and irritation is the result of a temper uncontrolled. The harmony in domestic circles often breaks by a hasty word and abusive language, how much better are they left unsaid. One smile of pleasure, one peaceful, appraising word spoken in the spirit of meekness, would be a power to sooth, to comfort and to bless.'[20]

An excellent poem by John K. Bangs goes like this:

If unkind words appear, file the thing away,
If some novelty jeers, file the thing away,
If some clever little bit of a sharp and pointed words
 with carrying a sting with it, file the thing away.

If some bits of gossip come, file the thing away,
If some scandalously spicy news comes, file the thing away,
If suspicion comes to you that, your neighbor isn't true,
let me tell you what to do file the thing away.
Do this for a little while, then go out and burn the file.

Revenge and getting even is not a principle of love. When we let angry spirit overcome our emotion, we lose objectivity and we become subjective. We become irrational and close-minded. We let the devil manage our soul. If one is a follower of Christ he cannot be sharp in dealing, he cannot be hard headed and devoid of sympathy. He cannot be coarse in his speech. He cannot be full of pomposity and self-esteem, he cannot be over beating nor can he use harsh word and censure and condemn.[21]   Let us learn from this Danish proverb, Kind words never wear out the tongue.·

Have you been destroying one another?

HOW NOT TO DESTROY ONE ANOTHER

- ❑ Never say I will avenge (Proverbs 24:29)
- ❑ Do not hate. If you hate you are a murderer (1John 3:15)
- ❑ Do not pay evil for evil (Romans 12:17)
- ❑ Do not do evil, it will return to you (Proverbs 17:13)
- ❑ Pray a fervent prayers it will help much (James 5:16)
- ❑ Put away all bitterness, anger and wrath (Eph. 4:31, 32)
- ❑ Do not befriend with angry furious men (Prov.. 22:24, 25)
- ❑ Remember bad company corrupts good character (1Corinthians15:33)
- ❑ Work on building people up not tearing down.
- ❑ Remember, God who reveals every secret (Daniel 2:28)
- ❑ Sincerely repent (1John 1:9)
- ❑ Do not make lies your refuge and hid under falsehood (Isaiah 28:15)
- ❑ Do not start trouble with rumors (Proverbs 16:28)
- ❑ Remember no rumor maker, no trouble (Proverbs 26:20)
- ❑ Walk upright (Psalms 15:2,3)
- ❑ Do what is good (John 12:35,36)

PRAYER

Dear Heavenly Father, I confess that at times I fall and am tempted to destroy Your child ___________. Teach me Father not to play God. Jesus, though He was God made Himself humble and lowly. I beg the Holy Spirit to direct my heart from any thought of destroying another but rather allow me in the spirit to building up others. This I pray in the name of Jesus Christ, my Lord. Amen.

AFFIRMATION

I have no right to destroy any person whom God loves and Christ died for. Being a child of God, I can accept any persecution and, by having a pure character in Jesus surely, I will win.

Love cannot exist without the
dimension of justice.

MELODY BEATTIE

To do injustice
is more disgraceful to suffer it.

PLATO

Execute Justice With One Another

FAIRPLAY
Express your opinion.

1. Justice to me is...___________________________________

____

—

2. Injustice to me is...___________________________________

____

3. In your dealings with one another you are...

Fair 10 9 8 7 6 5 4 3 2 1 Unfair

CONFER. Guide questions for discussion

1. Can you relate an experience of personal injustice?

2. Give reasons why man commits injustices to one another.

3. How should a Christian deal with injustice in all aspect of life?

4. What would you do if someone were unjust with you?

5. How do you confront someone who was impartial in his dealings?

6. Should Christians just keep silent and endure the injustices done to him? Should he fight back? Explain.

Marvin Marcelino

Execute Justice With One Another

...you truly execute justice with one another.
Jeremiah 7:5 RSV

Ene suffered injustice in the workplace. Upon his hiring in a company, he was promised all the benefits due him. Years past he was never been given privileges and benefits. His promotion to regular status was ignored. Not even a contract Rene could remember he signed. The management knew from the very beginning what Rene deserves. The management tricked Rene and kept from him his privileges and benefits.

Rendering justice to one another is one of the great pillars of love. Partiality in judging is not good ⟨Proverbs 24.23⟩ There are numerous outcries for justice in every corner of the world. The church is not exempted. Injustices are the battle cry of most victims, from denial of basic needs to the violation of human rights, added to this the corruptness of the justice system of humankind. Justice means impartiality, honesty, uprightness, evenhandedness, equality and fairness.

What is justice? It is offering honor and honesty not only to God but also to man ⟨2Corinthians 8.21⟩ Aristotle said, ·Justice is the only virtue that is regarded as someone else's good because it secures advantage for another person. Justice is not part of virtue but the whole of it.· Aristotle's study of justice points to two injustices. 1⟩ unlawful to anything contrary to the law, and 2⟩ unfair, the kind of things done at the expense of fairness or equality, both excess and defiant exhibit injustice.

The wise king tells us not to neglect an appeal for help from one who is in real need (Proverbs 21:13). Such a hard person can expect no sympathy when he is in trouble. His cry for help never acknowledged. He will be a victim of his own callousness and heartless attitude. A famous writer Ellen White wrote, In all business transactions, we are to let the light shine decidedly. Everything is to be done with strictness in integrity. We shall lose nothing in the end by fair dealing. We are to live the law of God in our words and perfect character after the divine similitude. All business, with those in the faith is to be transacted on righteous principle. Everything is to be seen in the light of God's law; everything done in fraud without duplicity, without thing of the guile.[22]

He who would take advantage of another's misfortune in order to benefit himself, or who seeks to profit himself through another's weakness or incompetence is the transgression of both principles of the precepts of the word of God.[23]

John Wesley reminds us, Do all good you can, in all the way you can, at all times you can with all the zeal for all the people you can while you can. Ellen White preached, If we possess the humility of our Maker we shall rise above the slights, the rebuffs, the annoyances of which we are daily exposed to, and they will cease to cast gloom over true spirit.[24] Plato taught, To do injustice is more disgraceful than suffer it. If our hearts are softened and subdued by the grace of Christ, and glowing with a sense of God's goodness and love, there will be a natural flow of love, sympathy, and tenderness to others.[25]

All acts of injustice are that tend to shorten light, the spirit, hatred and revenge, or the indulgence of any passion that leads to injurious act toward others, or causes us even to wish them harm. A self-neglect of caring for the needy or suffering all self-indulgences or unnecessary deprivation or excess labor that tends to injure health all these are, to a greater or less degree violation of the sixth commandments.[26] Psalm 58:2 states, in your heart you device injustice.· Did you know that the best portion of a good man's life is his little nameless, unremembered acts of kindness and love? The memory of the just is blessed, but the name of the wicked shall rot ₍Proverbs 10:7₎

Obedience to the law is necessary. Law is a pledge to do justice to one another. Percy Shelley said in his poem, *To the men of England*, ·The seed you sow, another reaps; the wealth ye find, another keeps; the robe you weave, another wears, the arms ye forge another bears. The effect of our work or anything we do will always have an impact upon others, which would be classified as fair or unfair.·

From Delilah to Samson, David to Uriah, Haman to Mordecai and the list continues, these people, one way or another executed justice to people they were involved. We can only look back to the stories and ask, Had Delilah, David and Haman been fair or unfair. It is worth learning from those who have done good or inappropriate justice. Charles Schwab said, ·Greatness lies in giving justice to others.·

Have you been fair with one another?

HOW TO EXECUTE JUSTICE TO ONE ANOTHER

-
- Persevere good judgments; avoid partiality (Proverbs 24:23).
- Apply due process; listen to both parties.
- Be fair even to the least who can't afford justice.
- Do not lead if you are unfair (Job 34:17).
- Do not be impartial to a wicked man or to deprive righteous man of justice (Proverbs 18:5).
- Do not look for self-interest but also of the interest of others (Philippians 2:4-5).
- Remember how God showed you to do justice (Micah 6:8).
- Provide honor to the Lord but also to man (2Corinthians 8:21).
- Execute true justice (Zechariah 7:9).
- Walk in integrity (Proverbs 10:9).
- Remember, partiality is not good (Proverbs 24:23).
- Exercise good conscience (Acts 24:16).
- To do justice is better than sacrifice (Proverbs 21:3).
- Do not show partiality, you commit sin (James 2:9).
- Do not sow injustice and reap calamity (Proverbs 22:8).
- Remember, deceitful and unmerciful is worthy of death (Romans 1:29,32).
- Attend to the sincere need of those who cry for justice (Jeremiah 5:28).

PRAYER

Dear Heavenly Father, I confess that I have been unjust with ____________. Teach me, Father, the way you execute justice with fair and lovingly. I beg the Holy Spirit to guide my heart to do justice with all fairness and love. This I pray in the name of Jesus Christ, my Lord and Savior, Amen.

AFFIRMATION

I must render justice to everyone in all my dealings because I am a channel of the love of God, who is fair and just.

Greed, anger and foolishness
are the roots of human woe,
to get rid of this observe love.

BHUDDIST PROVERB

There is no greater calamity than the lavish desire,
there is no greater guilt than discontentment,
and there is not greater disaster than greed.

LAO TZE

Do Not Envy One Another

GREED BREEDER

What do you envy most?

____

Comment on the following verses.

1. Psalms 37:1 Don't be annoyed by anyone who does wrong, and don't envy them. ·

____

2. Aeschylus Few men have the strength to honor a friend's success without
envy. ·_____________________________________

3. Ellen White Envy is like a row of hook to hang up grudges. ·

____

4. I say Envy is... _______________________________

____

1. Can you differentiate wants and needs?

2. Why do people become envious?

3. Differentiate the characteristics of a person in need and an envious person.

4. How would you treat a person who is envious about you?

5. How can a Christian overcome envy? Give some steps.

Do Not Envy One Another

Let us not be desirous...envying one another.
Galatians 5:26 KJV

n Greek history, a young man was so respected in public games that his fellow citizens raised a statue in his honor, to keep fresh the memory of his victories. The statue so excited the envy of another rival, who had been defeated in the races. One night he stole out under the cover of darkness with the intention to destroy the statue, but he only nicked it slightly. He then gave it a final heave, and it fell on top of him and killed him. True to the saying, that envy only hurts the one who is guilty of it.[27]

Terry Edwards' definition of envy is this, Envy is a feeling of jealousy and resentment that arises when we become aware that another person is enjoying an advantage or blessing that we wish was ours. Joshua Loth Liebman noted, It is not that he does not possess enough for his wants, but what other possesses more is that haunts him, makes him miserable with another's real achievements. This is the cancer eating his serenity. The wise man asks who can stand before envy' (Proverbs 27:4) Envy never says, I want what others have, but rather, it says, I wished others did not have what they have.

Where there is envy there will be disorder and vile practice. Most sin begins at the senses, but afterwards, Satan creeps into the heart. Envy also rots the bones (Proverbs 14:30) Selfishness according to French moralist, Francois de La Rochefoucauld, is the root of all natural moral evils.

He who is at peace with God and his fellowmen cannot be made miserable. Envy will not be in his heart; evil surmising will not find room there; hatred cannot exist. John Locke an English philosopher, said, Let not any one say he cannot govern his passion; nor hinder them from breaking out and carrying him to action. For what he can do before a prince or a great man, he can do alone or in the presence of God if he will.·

John Milton adds, He who reigns within himself and rules his passion, desires, and fears is more than a king.· ·The first and best victory is to conquer self and to be conquered by self is with all things the most shameful and vile.· Envy is the most despicable traits of satanic character. It is constantly seeking and the lifting up of self by casting slur upon others. A man who is envious will be little others, thinking to exalt himself..., he hate to praise another..., envy is the offering of pride, and this entertains the heart that will lead to cruel deeds of hatred, revenge and murder.·[28] Yes, envy can consume you⸗

Robert Leighton tracked the beginning of ruin by envy, noted, Sin is first pleasing then it grows away, then delightful, then frequent, then habitual, then confirmed, then the man is impenitent. Then he is resolved never to repeat and by then he is ruined.·

Do not confuse wants with needs; wants make the heart covet and complain and it drives one to crave for more and more. My crown is in my heart, not on my head. My crown is called content· William Shakespeare is simply saying that not every want is a need.

We fail to see that life is not accumulating things but in knowing God. Elizabeth of Thuringia wrote; We are made loveless by our possessions.· ·The secret of contentment,· Lin Yutang said, is to know how you enjoy what you have.·

Plato, a great philosopher, in 385 B.C., said, When we have not what we like, we must like what we have.· It means contentment does not come from having more, but in desiring less. Davids sin ripened beyond desire for pleasure, power, or possessions, at the expense of everything. Love seeks not its own it will not prompt men to seek their own ease and indulgence of self.·[29]

There are so many cases of envy recorded in the Bible starting with Cain to Abel (Genesis 4.4-8), Sarah and Hagar (Genesis 16.5, 6), Rachel and Leah (Genesis 30.1, 15), Josephs brothers (Genesis 77.4-11,18-20), Korah, Dathan,

Abiram and Moses (Numbers 16:3). Indeed, covetousness is one of the common and popular sins of the last days and has a paralyzing influence upon the soul.[30]

Have you been envying one another?

HOW NOT TO ENVY ONE ANOTHER

❑ Do not covet anything from thy neighbor (Exodus 20:17)

❑ Remember all good gift comes from the Father (Jas 1:17)

❑ Do not envy (1Corinthians 13:4)

❑ Jealousy kills the simple. (Job 5:2)

❑ If God has clothed the grass…will He not much do to you? (Matthew 6:30)

❑ Ask God to supply all your needs according to His riches (Psalms 4:19)

❑ Rid yourself of…envy (1Peter 2:1)

❑ Let your conversation be without covetousness (Heb. 13:5)

❑ Be contented with what you have (Acts 20:33)

❑ Behave properly without envy (Romans 13:13)

❑ Remember covetousness is idolatry (Colossians 3:5)

❑ Bear in mind, being full of envy is worthy of death (Romans 1:29-32)

❑ Stop desiring richness that brings destruction (1 Tim. 6:10)

❑ Do not enrich yourself but be poor before God (Luke 12:21)

❑ Think. Neither silver nor gold can save us from Lord's wrath (Zephaniah 1:18)

❑ Honor God with what you have (Proverbs 3:9)

❑ Do not be lover of self and covetousness. (2Timothy 3:2)

PRAYER

Dear Heavenly Father, I confess that I was envious of _____________. Teach me Father to be content with what I have. Jesus slept with no soft pillow, but I have. I beg the Holy Spirit to direct my eyes and heart away from earthly possessions and towards heavenly riches. Teach me to look at the deprived people and learn from their contentment. This I pray in the name of Jesus Christ, my Lord and Savior. Amen.

AFFIRMATION

I have all God has given godliness, spiritual blessings and all that pertains to life eternal. He is sufficient and I am content.

Whom we love best
to them we can say least.

BOB PHILIPS

Dont judge any man until
you have walked two moons in his moccasins.

NATIVE AMERICAN PROVERB

Judge Not One Another

VERDICT DROPPER

What do you hate most in other people?

____

Which of these can you do?

______ ·Search seven times before you suspect anyone·
Chinese Proverbs

______ ·Judge not according to appearance... ·John 7:24

______ ·Avoid speculating· 1Timothy 4:7

______ ·Judge not by eyes and ears· Isaiah 11:3

CONFER. Guide questions for discussion

1. Why do people jump to conclusions about others?

2. How can you reconcile both telling the truth and judging? Can you see any difference?

3. Explain why comparing can be a form of judging.

4. How can we avoid judging?

5. How can one be honest to another without being judgmental?

Judge Not One Another

Let us stop passing judgment on one another.
Romans 14:13 NIV

An attractive woman with three children moved into a small town. A few weeks later, she was the most talked-about woman among the community. Several men always visit her. She was a poor housekeeper and her children always running in the streets. She spent most of her time lying on the sofa. Such was the conversation among the neighbors. One morning, the widow collapsed in the post office, and the truth came out. She was suffering from an incurable disease and could not do housework. She sent the children away, for them not to see her in pain, her old family doctor, lawyer, and her husband's brother were her frequent visitors. The town became kind to her for the remaining months of her life.[31]

Fenelon a French churchman, noted, It is through our own imperfection which makes us respond to the imperfections of others; a sharp-sight, self-love of our own which cannot pardon the self-love of others. Our own faults and imperfections help us see the faults of others that are sometimes fabricated. To judge means; is to accuse, to condemn, to presume, to regard, to opine, to suppose, to ascertain, to criticize and to determine.

God never gave man the right to judge (Matthew 7:1) When we judge, we say we have no sin, and when we say we are clean of sin, we very are wrong (1John 1:8; Proverbs 21:2)

Judging is like standing on a slippery ground next to conclusion (1Corinthian 10:12) We cannot see a man's motive and heart and who are we to judge another (James 4:12)

Benjamin Disraeli observed, It is much easier to be critical than to be correct. We are quick to jump into negative conclusion about people. We say things about people with evil motive that may not be even true. It is safe for us to have all

Marvin Marcelino

the facts first before we speak to guard us of any malicious judgment. Often the mistake of prejudging others backfires and places one in embarrassment. Filipinos have a proverb that states, ·A thief hates another thief, or a gossiper hates the like.· Do we hate people who behave like our self?

Jesus said, ·How one judges another similarly how one will be judged by God.· That means never set oneself as the standard of measurement. Never make ones opinion, views of duty, interpretation of scripture a criterion for others and in ones heart condemn them if they do not come up to your ideals.

We cannot read the heart. ·We are faulty; we are not qualified to sit judgment upon others. Faulty man can only judge by the outer appearance. His God love who knows every spring of action, and who deal tenderly and compassionately, is given to decide the case of every soul.·[32]

The poem *Don't Judge* by S.G. Miraflores captures the essence of judgment.

> *Do not judge a man by the clothes he wears.*
> *God made the one, the tailor made the other.*
>
> *Don't judge a man by his family relations,*
> *Cain belonged to the best family.*
>
> *Don't judge a man by his speech, A parrot can talk*
> *A Tongue is but an instrument of sound.*
>
> *Don't judge a man by his failures in life,*
> *many a man who failed whom*
> *God exalted to the highest...*

To avoid being judgmental, here is what St. Augustine taught, ·If two friends ask you to judge a dispute, don't accept, because you will lose one friend.· Wayn Dyer said, ·When you judge another, you do not define them, you define yourself.· Lastly, may our aim in life be like Jeanne Moreaus ·My aim in life is not to judge.· Will you give it a thought before you cast judgment upon each other?

Have you been judging one another?

HOW NOT TO JUDGE ONE ANOTHER

- ❑ Do not covet anything from thy neighbors (Exodus 20:17).
- ❑ Ask. Who made you a judge (Acts 7:27)?
- ❑ Do not judge not or you will be judged (Luke 6:37).
- ❑ Do not judge not according to appearance (John 7:24).
- ❑ Remember when you judge you are doing the same thing (Romans 2:1).
- ❑ Bear in mind that God is a judge Himself (Psalms 50:6).
- ❑ Judge not by what the eyes see and ear can only hear (Isaiah 11:3).
- ❑ Acknowledge your sins and not of others.
- ❑ Open your heart to the Holy Spirit.
- ❑ Examine ourselves first.
- ❑ Think only of pure, noble, lovely about your neighbors (Philippians 4:8).
- ❑ Walk in the Spirit (Galatians 5:16).
- ❑ Avoid speculations (1Timothy 4:7).
- ❑ We are guilty if we speak evil of man (Titus 3:2,3).
- ❑ Do not allow ma to judge you (Colossians 2:16).
- ❑ Remember there is only one lawgiver...who are you to judge another? (James 4:12).
- ❑ Wait until the Lord comes and will bring to light hidden things (1Corinthians 4:5).

PRAYER

Dear Heavenly Father, I admit I was too rash judging ___________. Teach me Father not to play God, for I am not created to be such. Jesus, though He was a God, made Himself humble and lowly. He did not condemn me, but the sin in me. I beg the Holy Spirit to guide my heart from having any judgmental thought and jumping to conclusions about and against another. This I pray in the name of Jesus Christ, my Lord and Savior. Amen.

AFFIRMATION

I have no right to judge others for God forbids me so. I am to pass love, not judgment to anybody.

Whoever takes delight in complaining will always find something to complain about.

JEREMIS GOTTHELF

Really, to stop criticism one must die.

VOLTAIRE

Do Not Grumble With One Another

COMPLAINT DESK
1. Write the names of people whom you have complained about and explain why.

Name   Reason

__________   _____________________

__________   _____________________

__________   _____________________

__________   _____________________

__________   _____________________

2. Other peoples complaints about you.

1. Why do people grumble with one another?

2. What is the right way to complain?

3. How should a Christian receive complaints against him? Give examples.

4. Is there such a thing as constructive complaint?

82

Marvin Marcelino

5. How would you deal with or confront a chronic
    complainer?

Do Not Grumble With One Another

Do not grumble with one another.
Romans 14:13 NIV

Charles Darwin was a chronic complainer, and was happiest when he had something to gripe. One night, he and his wife were guests at a banquet, where everything was wrong. The speeches were dry; the food was inferior; the service even more so, and worst of all, the naturalist was given a draft about which he had a phobia. Throughout the meal, he grumbled and swore.

Later, the sponsor of the affair came over to Mrs.. Darwin and said apologetically, ʻI do hope your husband will forgive us. We wanted so much for him to have a good time.· He had such a wonderful time,· she assured the host. He was able to find fault with everything.ʼ[33]

Grumbling is never a character of love. To grumble is to murmur, repine; it is an expression of discontent and faultfinding, grievance or lament. Everywhere oneʼs head turns there are always sounds of whine, murmur, complaint, discontentment, grievance or faultfinding. People do not run out of something to grumble. Most of these grumbles are not contained to one person; it passes commonly from one person to another. When one entertains or listens, one become like the grumbler.

Do you know a person who is exceedingly satisfied with his environment or with the people he works with or the life he is living? Who has strife, who has complaints? ʻ(Proverbs 23:29)

Everybody always finds something minute or major issues to grumble. Surprisingly we advertise our grumbling for sympathy from other, and we seek those who will patronize our sentiments. Is not this a familiar tactic

Marvin Marcelino

Satan used in Heaven when he was able to recruit one third of the angels? ·There is in a man a disposition to esteem himself highly than his brother, to work for self, to seek the highest place and after this result in evil surmising, and bitterness of spirit.·[34]

·Bitterness and animosity must be banished from the soul if we are to be in harmony with heaven.·[35] ·Instead of allowing jealousy or evil surmising into our hearts, why not go to the person and frankly but kindly settle before them the things you have heard harmful to their character and influence and pray for them.·[36]

·Let everyone behave, unsetting the fruits of others, by sowing seed of envy, jealousy and grumbling, for God hear words and judges not by assertion…, but the fruits of one·s course of action.·[37] True love to our fellowmen is an evidence of our love to God.

·Our faith may lead us to give our bodies to be sacrificed, yet without sacrificing love, such as love in the bosom of Jesus that was exemplified in His life we are a sounding brass and a tinkling cymbal.·[38]

Let no murmur and complaint come from your lips; remember that angels hear them.·[39] A Jewish proverb tells us, ·If men thanked God for good things, they would not have time to complain about the bad.·

I like George E. Taylor·s comment about complaining; he said, ·The reason we criticize and condemn other people is that their methods of sinning are different from ours.·What we hate of others is what we are.

A pastor kept a special notebook labeled *Complaints of Church Members Against Other Members.*· When someone would tell him faults of another member, he would say, ·Here·s my complaint book; I·ll write down what you say and you sign it. Then when I have to take out the matter officially, I shall know and expect you to testify too.· The effect· the pastor had opened the book many times and no entry was made.·[40] ·Realize that if you have time to whine and complain about something then you have the time to do something about it,· reminds Anthony J. D·Angelo.

Do you grumble against one another?

HOW TO AVOID GRUMBLING WITH ONE ANOTHER

- ❑ Think only positive thoughts about your neighbor (Philippians 4:8).

- ❑ Do not envy anything that belongs to your neighbors (Exodus 20:17).

- ❑ Remember that your body is destroyed in groaning (Psalms 32:3).

- ❑ Remember that God looks at the heart not on the outward appearance. (1Samuel 16:7).

- ❑ Do not contend with the Almighty by faultfinding (Job 40:2).

- ❑ Bear in mind that the mouth of the wicked gushes evil (Proverbs 15:28).

- ❑ Exercise wisdom by holding your tongue (Proverbs 10:19).

- ❑ Guard your mouth to preserve your life (Proverbs 13:3).

- ❑ Do not be overcome by anxiety (Proverbs 12:25).

- ❑ Do not speak too many unnecessary words (Proverbs 10:19).

PRAYER

Dear Heavenly Father, I confess that I always grumble against ____________ about ________________. Help me Father to overcome this weakness in me. Jesus came to earth but never grumbled at anything or about anyone. I beg the Holy Spirit to direct my heart to be more understanding with others. This I pray in the name of Jesus Christ, my Lord and Savior. Amen.

Marvin Marcelino

AFFIRMATION

I am a loving person, mature enough to understand the limitations of another. If ever I have to complain, I will say it with love.

Love is to risk not being loved in return…
dont love to be loved in return.
Leo Buscaglia

Anybody can be a heart specialist.
The only requirement is loving one another.
Angie Papadakis

Care For One Another

CONFRONT.

CARETAKER Fill in the blanks.

1. People I care for. ___________________________________
   Why? ___________________________________

2. People I seldom care for. ___________________________________
   Why? ___________________________________

3. People I occasionally care for. ___________________________________
   Why? ___________________________________

4. People I totally do not care for. ___________________________________
   Why? ___________________________________

5. People I will never care for.___________________________________
   Why? ___________________________________

6. Evaluate your responses on numbers 1-5, give 3 good reasons for each, and examine why your attitude is such.

CONFER. *Guide questions for discussion*

1. Why should we care for one another?
2. Is it okay to be choosy with whom we need to care for?
3. What are the characteristics of a caring Christian? Give examples.
4. How do you define the word caring?
5. How do you deal with not-so-caring people?

Care For One Another

Care for one another. I Corinthians 12:25 RSV

Awealthy businessman was driving along the highway when he collided with a truck. He was hospitalized for some weeks. In the meantime, his wife had received a half dozen letters of condolences from the people who heard that she lost her husband. She was upset because he was very much alive. She gave the letters to her husband, and one thing struck him. There was hardly a word about the husband, everything was about her, and no one seemed to miss him. It did not make much difference whether he was around or not.

·Too many of us stay walled up,· said Eleanor Roosevelt because we are afraid of being hurt. We are afraid to care too much; for fear that the other person does not care at all.·

Caring is a form of loving. Caring is personal. The Greek word *epilomei* means to involve forethought and provisions; it indicates the mind towards the object of care. It involves doing whatever is necessary to provide care for someone. Caring is an act of concern, which may come in different forms. Similarly, understood as to adore, to prize, to reassure, to respect, to foster, to have a concern or to mind.

The word care is loaded with responsibility. It expects total commitment. A famous writer wrote, ·The talent to care is the most underrated talent God gave. Caring, loving, and nurturing has a value that transcends the high portals that put people in the spotlight.·

A caring heart, a listening ear, a thoughtful word, a gentle touch will help lift the heavy heart of every soul along life's road. It is the thoughtful consideration that God values.·[41]

Love is an act of will while caring is an attitude of the mind or direction of the will which seeks nothing but the good of

Marvin Marcelino

another. Caring is giving respect to others. Caring is offering support and compliment, caring in understanding people, caring is being sensitive to the needs of others, and caring is an active personal sacrifice for the sake of another.

Caring is a 24-hour-a-day duty. It requires the whole heart. Care is freely given; it is not asking anything in return. Caring does not spoil one or abuse another. Charlotte Lunsford said, ·We will not always know whose lives we touched and made better for having cared, because actions can sometimes have unforeseen ramifications. What is important is that you care, and you act.·

·There is nothing more valuable in life·, said Lee Atwater, ·than human beings; nothing sweeter than human touch.· In caring, we should not work in the standpoint of duty merely but from love because Christ died for their salvation. Christ has purchased these souls, and they need our care, and He expects us to love them, He loves us in our sin and waywardness. Love is the agency through which God work to draw the heart to Him.·[42]

Queen Elizabeth of Hungary gave alms and advice to the poor. She said, ·Give also to the poor like you.· We do not have more.· A woman among the crowd said, ·What are we going to give?· The queen replied, ·If one does not have money, but you have a heart, eyes, feet, and lips, you can use it for good of poor.·[43]

Yes, every day is a good day to lose oneself to others, and anytime is a good time to see humanity as brothers. It is good to care for others regardless of color, race, religion, or creed. Now you understand that caring is a continuous service of love. Lastly, Theodore Roosevelt reminds everyone, ·Nobody cares how much you know until they know how much you care.·

Have you been caring for one another?

HOW TO CARE FOR ONE ANOTHER

- ❑
- ❑ Open your heart wide to your brother (Deuteronomy 15:11)
- ❑ Do not close your heart to your brother (1John 3:17)
- ❑ Let your caring be seen by God and men (2Corinthians 7:12)
- ❑ Be interested in the other person.
- ❑ Be aware of anothers needs.
- ❑ Be a human being.
- ❑ Be supportive.

PRAYER

Dear Heavenly Father, I confide that I am not that caring to ____________. Help me, Father, to be more caring like Jesus. He cares so much that he even gave His life for me and saved me from the curse of sin. I beg the Holy Spirit to direct my heart to be more caring for others. This I pray in the name of Jesus Christ, my Lord and Savior. Amen.

AFFIRMATION

I am a caring person, because God cares for me. God gives me another chance to let this Holy Love manifest through me. I will care for everyone regardless of status, religion, creed, race and color, for I am a child of Love.

God has given us two hands –
one to receive with and the other to give with.

BILLY GRAHAM

A hand not extended in giving is
in no position to receive.

ARTHUR C. FRANTZREB

Do Not Refuse One Another

HOLDER FOLDER Are you a Holder Folder? Honestly, encircle where you believe you are now.

No.		Scale	
1.	Helpful	10 9 8 7 6 5 4 3 2 1	Not helpful
2.	Thoughtful	10 9 8 7 6 5 4 3 2 1	Forgetful
3.	Open-minded	10 9 8 7 6 5 4 3 2 1	Close-minded
4.	Motivator	10 9 8 7 6 5 4 3 2 1	Manipulator
5.	Expressive	10 9 8 7 6 5 4 3 2 1	Secretive
6.	Just	10 9 8 7 6 5 4 3 2 1	Unjust
7.	Promoter	10 9 8 7 6 5 4 3 2 1	Demoter
8.	Transparent	10 9 8 7 6 5 4 3 2 1	Opportunist
9.	Fair	10 9 8 7 6 5 4 3 2 1	Unfair
10.	Provider	10 9 8 7 6 5 4 3 2 1	Depriver

CONFER. Guide questions for discussion

1. Should Christians refuse or deprive one another of the benefit one is entitled to? Examples. jobs, just wages, rights, etc.?

2. When should one be deprived of his rights and benefits?

3. How can one be deprived of his rights? Give examples.

4. What actions should a Christian make if he knows he is being deprived of his rights?

Marvin Marcelino

5. How would you confront one who is manipulatively depriving another of his rights?

Do Not Refuse One Another

Do not refuse one another. I Corinthians 7.5 RSV

braham Lincoln was paying one of his frequent visits to a hospital for soldiers. He would walk from ward to ward, cheering and sympathizing with the patients. He came to the bedside of a young soldier who was dying, and asked, ·Well, my boy, what can I do for you?· The lad looked up and expressed a wish, ·Will you write my mother for me?· ·That I will,·Abraham Lincoln agreed and called for a paper and pen. He sat down beside the cot and wrote what the young man dictated. Finished, he turned to the boy and said, ·I'll mail this from my office as soon as I get back, and now is there anything else I can do?· The boy looked up, hesitated, and finally blurted out, ·Could you stay with me, I want you to hold my hand.· Lincoln did until the young man died hours later.[44]

To refuse in this section means to deny, and to deprive is to take away something from, to keep from using, to curtail, to rob, to cut off, to strip off, and to prohibit or to hinder. All of it ends in taking something equally important from another person. How does one deprive another? Deprivation is holding back from somebody the rights to freedom, happiness, expression, opportunity, promotion, success, education, wage increase, and most of all love. Mahatma Gandhi said, ·To deprive a man of his natural liberty and to deny him of ordinary amenities of life is worse than starving the body; it is starving of the soul, and dweller of the body.· We may be able to refuse and deprive others now, but that will not be for long, for God is a God of justice and fairness.

Marvin Marcelino

The book *Christ's Object Lessons,* by Ellen White, said, 'We should anticipate the sorrows, the difficulties, and the trouble of others. We should enter in to their joys and cares of both high and low, rich and poor, Christ said freely you received; freely you give.'(Matthew 10:18)

'God has given us two hands,' said Billy Graham, 'one to receive and the other to give with.' Poor souls, like many of us, are exhausted and ready to give up. We need sympathetic words and encouragement. There are orphans whom Christ has bidden his followers to receive as a trust from God. Too often, these orphans passively neglected, or intentionally ignored.

Under privileged people may be ragged, disrespectful and seemingly unappealing in every way, yet they are God's property bought with a price, and they are as precious in His eye as you are. They are members of God's great family, only they do not know, and you being Christian stewards, are responsible for them. Their souls, God said He would require at your hands.

I came across an article entitled, *How and when to say no.* It talks about how to refuse a request. How discreet should one be in refusing a request? The article said, 'If it makes you feel good, it is your own making. If it makes them feel good, it is only their good you are thinking. Refuse for one's good and all.'

The bottom line: is deprivation is subtle and played by canny and wily minds that are simply running away from responsibility. The leaders' delaying tactics·in giving what is due their subordinates. The legal parlance has an adage that says, 'Justice delayed is justice denied.'

'The church is greatly deficient in love and humanity. Many are preserved cold, chilling, and an iron dignity that repels those who are brought to their influence.· Barbara Hand Herra preached that, giving frees us from the familiar territory of our needs by opening our minds to the unexplored worlds occupied by the needs of others.·

·A refusing spirit is contagious. It creates an atmosphere that is withering to good impulses and good resolves. It chokes the natural current of human sympathy, cordiality and love. Under its influence, people become constrained, and their social and generous attributes are destroyed for want of exercise.[45] H. Jackson Brown Jr. concludes never deprive someone of hope; it might be all they have.·

Have you been depriving blessings of each other?

HOW NOT TO REFUSE ONE ANOTHER

- ❑ Never reject people God never did ⟨Romans 11.1⟩
- ❑ Do not insist your own ideas ⟨1Corinthians 13.5⟩
- ❑ Bear all things ⟨1Corithians 13.7⟩
- ❑ Give every man what is due him ⟨Romans 13.7⟩
- ❑ Think only of the good of others ⟨1Corinthians 10.24, 31-33⟩
- ❑ Carry others' burdens ⟨Galatians 6.2⟩
- ❑ Take to mind the interest of others ⟨Philippians 2.4⟩
- ❑ Please your neighbor ⟨Romans 15.1, 2⟩
- ❑ Supply the needs of others ⟨Acts 20.33, 34⟩
- ❑ Do unto others what you others do unto you ⟨Matthew 7.12⟩

PRAYER

Dear Heavenly Father, I admit that at times I deprive ___________ of __________ which he/she is entitled to. Help me, Father, to be more considerate of others. Jesus came to earth, yet He did not deprive me of the privilege of salvation. I

beg the Holy Spirit to direct my heart to be more caring and understanding of others. This I pray in the name of Jesus Christ, my Lord and Savior. Amen.

AFFIRMATION

I am considerate and caring. Gods love compels me to love those who are in need, for I am a child of a provident God.

Wherever the love of Jesus reigns
there is peace and rest.
ELLEN G. WHITE

With all thy faults. I love thee still.

WILLIAM COWPER

Be At Peace With One Another

PEACEKEEPING FORCE
Fill in the blanks.

1. As a peacekeeper, I am to…

____

2. For peace to be maintained I am to…

____

3. I pledge to keep peace by…

____

4. At any conflict within my reach, I will…

____

5. I will never exchange peace with…

____

CONFER. Guide questions for discussion

1. What is peace to you personally?

2. For what reason/s would peace not exist between two people?

3. How can one maintain peace? (At home, school workplace and church.)

4. With whom should peace start? With others or self?

5. What is not peace to one another? Give examples.

Be At Peace With One Another

...be at peace with one another. Mark 9.50 RSV

D r. Oppenheimer, the supervisor of the atomic bomb project appeared before the congressional committee. When asked if the world had any defense against nuclear weapons, he surprisingly responded, ⅂ can certainly have one.· The room suddenly stood still, his expectant audience attentively tune in on him. The physicist looked over them with a hush and added softly, ·The one defense that the world will always have is PEACE.[46]

Blessed are the peacemakers ⟨Matthew 5.9⟩ Peace has many forms - accord, harmony, agreement, conciliation, order, accommodation, repose, contentment, and love for each other. Paul advocated peace when he said, ⅃et us therefore, make every effort to do what leads to peace and mutual edification· ⟨Romans14.19⟩

Paul was a former member of the Sanhedrin, whose work dealt with studying the merits of each case presented. Paul was an expert on settling issues based on merits. He was ready when he settled some issues in the churches he worked. This time, however, Paul was different. He was no longer the old Saul; he was now more concerned with bringing peace ⟨a harmonious relationship between persons⟩ to every member of the church.

·Make every effort,·means all effort must be done to ensure peace between two conflicting people. No effort is limited in order for peace to prevail. We have to have a sacrificing spirit.

That is by being patient with the weak ₋whatever insults you receive take them as insults to Christ ⟨Romans 15.3⟩ Ask the Spirit for endurance and encouragement just for guidance to unity. Isaiah said, ⅃et him have perfect peace whose mind is in God₋⟨Isaiah 26.3⟩⟨Galatians 5.22⟩

Marvin Marcelino

Perhaps peace in these last days will be the most expensive commodity ever to acquire. Jose Rizal, patriot and national hero of the Philippines, sent a letter to Graciano Lopez Jaena (another Philippine patriot) in Paris in March of 1889. The letter said, 'Union, goodwill and good feeling, these are what we need.' 'A secure stable peace,' Dean Acheson said, 'is not a goal we can reach all at once. It is a dynamic state produce by efforts and faith, with justice and courage.'

The struggle for peace is continuous and hard. The prize is never ours, and it is true that the only persons who will ever benefit are the people who produce peace. Albert Einstein preached, 'Peace cannot be kept by force; it can only be kept by understanding.' If only man would be more open-minded, understanding and considerate, there could be no conflict. There would be a lot of room for understanding and consideration and of love. Another author added, 'Peace can be enjoyed if meekness and love are both exercised.'

Yes, love is the only solution. No debate is needed to find peace, love is the supreme antidote to any conflict, and no other but Jesus the Son of God has proven it. Where God is, there is peace. Mother Theresa noted, 'If we have no peace, it is because we have forgotten that we belong to each other.'

Are you at peace with everybody? If you are not, go and be a peacemaker! There are five enemies to peace: avarice, ambition, envy, anger, and pride. We need to vanquish these enemies. 'Cultivate the Love of Christ; it should well up from the soul of the Christian *or anyone* like streams in the deserts, refreshing and beautifying bringing gladness, peace and joy into his own life and the lives of others.[47]

Are you contributing to peace?

HOW TO BE AT PEACE WITH ONE ANOTHER

- ❑ Do not forget the laws and commandments of God.
- ❑ Be spiritually minded (Romans 8:6)
- ❑ Preach the gospel of peace (Rom. 10:15)
- ❑ Be a person of understanding (Proverbs 11:12)
- ❑ Please the Lord and He will make your enemies be at peace with you (Proverbs 16:7)
- ❑ Hold your peace; you are counted as wise (Proverbs 17:28)
- ❑ Love at all times (Proverbs 17:17)
- ❑ Endure all things (1Corinthians 13:7)
- ❑ Be a peacemaker (Matthew 5:9)
- ❑ Live peaceably with all men (Romans 12:18)
- ❑ Conquer all with love. (Proverbs 10:12)

PRAYER

Dear Heavenly Father, I admit that I am not at peace with ____________. Help me, Father, to be more understanding and forgiving like You. Jesus Christ, Your very Son, came to bring love and peace to rule the earth but I am destroying His work. I beg the Holy Spirit to guide my heart to be at peace with others. This I pray in the name of Jesus Christ, my Lord and Savior. Amen.

AFFIRMATION

I am a peacemaker. I am a peacekeeping force. I am at peace with others and myself. I am an advocate of love. I am to offer peace to everyone regardless of status, religion, creed, race, and color for I am a child of a peace-loving God.

A truth thats told with bad intent,
beats all the lies you can invent.
ROBERT BLAKE

This is the punishment of a liar,
he is not believed even when he speaks the truth
BABYLONIAN TALMUD

Do Not Lie To One Another

HONEST LIAR
Tick three from each column.

1. My lying habit is...
   - remarkably at its worst
   - a necessary evil
   - done when deemed necessary
   - my way of life
   - only when I really need something

2. In order for me to stop lying...
   - I need a seminar
   - I need help
   - I need direction
   - please cut my tongue
   - I would die first

3. Matters I lied about...___________________________________
4. People I lied to ___________________________________

CONFER. Guide questions for discussion

1. Why do people tell a lie?

2. When is a lie being morally correct?

3. Is there such a thing as white lie? Explain.

4. How do you know if a person is lying?

5. How would you confront a lying Christian?

Do Not Lie To One Another

Do not lie to one another. Colossians 3.9 RSV

A priest saw a group of little boys sitting in a circle with a dog in the middle. He asked them what they were doing with the dog. One lad said, 'We are not doing anything with the dog; we are just telling lies, and the one who tells the biggest lie gets the dog. The priest told them that he was shocked, and preached that telling lies were terribly bad. To close his sermon, he said that when he was a little boy, like them, he had never even thought of telling a lie. Then one little boy stood up and said, 'Okay fellas, let us give him the dog.'

It is written on stone, 'Thou shall not bear false witness' (Exodus 8.16). The law of God says, 'Do not tell a lie.' David supports this principle when he said, 'He who utters lies to his neighbor with flattering lips and a double heart they speak.' (Psalms 12.2) If one confesses that, he just could not stop lying, this only confirms that everyone is a liar (Psalm 116.11) because we were born as such (Psalms 58. 3), with which makes our heart deceitful (Jeremiah 17.9). Even then, that does not give us a license to lie; it is telling us that it is the sin within us, which makes us lie to each other.

To tell a lie is not to tell the truth. To tell a lie is to distort the truth, either by removing a word or dot or by adding another word. Can you remember the tactics the Serpent used to deceive Eve in the Garden of Eden? The Lord gave His warning through prophet Jeremiah that; man will be deceitful, his tongue will be taught to speak lies, and man is weary to repent (Jeremiah 9:3-9)

A liar may either be one who enjoys lying for his own sake, or one who is striving to gain glory of profit. There are many forms of lying, namely, manipulative lying, impersonal lying, benevolent lying, status lying, cover-up lying, conspiracy lying, decoy lying, falsehood, misleading statements, and misrepresentations. Dennis Diderot is right, We swallow greedily any lie that flatters us, but we sip little at a truth we find bitter.

Have you had a society in which all truth was blindly exposed would be more like hell than paradise, where not speaking the truth is a duty. Compromised truth will not cause pain to others for kindness or brotherhood sake. To Filipinos, telling the truth against a friend is tantamount to *walang pakikisama* or betrayal. That is just a fact, Donald Rumsfeld said, there are a lot of people who lie and get away with it.

Why do we lie? We lie to save a face rather than face the shame. We lie to survive; we lie to live. We lie to be rich; we lie to gain. We lie to please others; we lie to be accepted and belong. We lie for others to believe. Doing these lying before God is suicide - spiritual suicide. Some men do fear to lie to their fellow man, but they have been taught and the restraining spirit of God has impressed them that it is fearful to lie to God.[48] Let your life be free from deceitful practices. Let no guile be found in your life. Shall anyone who claims to be the son or daughter of God, give himself up to deceitful practices and lying?[49]

Lying and being honest is a choice. In many cases, moral powers seemed deadened, and it is difficult to arouse them to a sense of the grievous nature of sin; they slip easily into the habits of prevarication, deceit and then lying.[50] Deceit brings its own disintegration of the soul to the deceiver, often hurting him more than the deceived… lying tends to break down the unity of unity; deceit seeks one member against another.[51]

Daniel Webster construes that half a fact is a whole falsehood.·Falsehood not only disagrees with truth, but usually quarrels among them.· Falsehood does not stay long hidden. An old Latin adage says, ·*Veritum dies aperit*·, which means, ·Time discloses the truth.·

Let one be truthful not to remain in the sin of lying. The Bible is clear that if we lie, then, we are the children of the Father of Lies·(John 8:44, 55), and liars are ungodly (1Timothy 1:10), and they will be burned in the lake of fire (Revelation 21:8)·

Have you been lying to one another?

HOW NOT TO LIE TO ONE ANOTHER

- ❑ Remember that God chose you and ordained you (John 15:16)
- ❑ Remember that you are a royal priesthood (1Peter 2:9)
- ❑ Remember that lying lips are an abomination to the Lord (Proverbs 12:19)
- ❑ Do not lie to one another (Leviticus 19:11)
- ❑ Do not bear false witness (Exodus 20:16)
- ❑ Do not listen to the haughty tongue (1John 4:20)
- ❑ Remember that he who speaks lies will perish. (Proverbs 19:7)
- ❑ Remember that he that speaks lies will not escape (Proverbs 19:5)
- ❑ Bear in mind that no one who lies will stand before God. (Psalms 101:7)
- ❑ Think that the Lord will be against you if you lie (Ezekiel 1:8)
- ❑ Never believe a lie (1Thessalonians 4:3)
- ❑ Walk in honesty (Romans 13:13)
- ❑ Speak for Christ (2Corinthians 2:17)
- ❑ Be guarded in truth (1 John 4:20)
- ❑ Speak the truth in the spirit of love (Ephesians 4:15)

PRAYER

Dear Heavenly Father, I confide that I lied to ____________ about ________________. Help me, Father, to overcome this weakness. Give me the courage to speak the truth though may break friendship or deny me riches. I beg the Holy Spirit to guide my lips from lying. This I pray in the name of Jesus Christ, my Lord Savior. Amen.

AFFIRMATION

I am to uphold the truth and tell nothing but the truth for I am a child of the God of Truth.

Any fool can criticize, condemn,
and complain and most fools do.

DALE CARNEGIE

If you win all your arguments,
you'll end up with no friends.

BOB PHILLIPS

Have No Lawsuit Against One Another

SWEET SOUR SUITS Complete the sentence.

1. For me, lawsuits are…

____

2. I will sue because of…

____

3. Giving up my privilege to sue means…

____

4. Your main reason for getting lawsuit is…(check one or more)

⭐⭐ hate because

______   ______________________

⭐⭐ revenge because

______   ______________________

⭐⭐ selfishness because

______   ______________________

⭐⭐ envy because

______   ______________________

⭐⭐ getting even because

______   ______________________

⭐⭐ greed because

____

CONFER. *Guide questions for discussion*

1. What good reasons one must have to engage in a lawsuit against another?

2. Is it necessary for Christians to go to court to settle differences?

3. Does winning a lawsuit make a Christian more honest and righteous than his rival?

4. What should you do to avoid settling differences in courts?

5. How should a Christian react when sued?

Have No Lawsuit Against One Another

*To have lawsuits at all with one another
Is defeat for you. 1Corinthians 6.7 RSV*

Once, a newspaper published some insulting things about a man who was trying to start a movement which he believed would benefit his fellow citizens. He went to a wise old man who often had things of this nature printed about him. ·What shall I do?· Shaking with rage and thrusting the paper before the old man, he asked, ·Shall I sue the paper?· Shall I fight the writer? Shall I place an advertisement in the paper denying it?· The old man answered quietly, ·Dont do anything.· ·But think all the people who will be talking about me when they read that.· I am thinking of them,· said the older man. ·Do you see that article? Well, half of those who saw it read the headlines only. Half of those who read the article never heard of you, and do not care about you one way or the other. Half of those who care one way or the other did not believe it, and half of those did believe it would forget all about it and you tomorrow. How many people do you think are left to do all that talking?·

To file lawsuits against each other means to blame, to indict, and to accuse another. This sickness was rampant in the days of Paul particular among the church members. ·The very fact that you have lawsuits among you means you were defeated already. Why not rather be wronged? Why cheat? Be assured the unrighteous ·your accusers· will not inherit the kingdom of God· ·1Corinthians 6.7-9· Try to be like Benjamin Franklin who said, ·I will speak ill of no man, not even in the matter of truth; just rather excuse the

Marvin Marcelino

faults I hear and upon proper occasions speak all the good I know of everybody.·

The Bible is clear when it says, ·If anyone wants to sue you and take away your tunic, let him have your cloak also· ·Matthew 5.40.41). Even if someone takes you to court, let him win. You did not lose because he won. Even if, he brings the case to all the courts on earth and you lost, yet you won in heaven. Those who sue you may celebrate today, but you will have your turn to rejoice in heaven. ·Satan is constantly sowing distrust, alienation, malice among God·s people. We shall often be tempted to feel that our rights are violated. Where there is no real cause for such feeling..., contentions, strife, and lawsuit between are disgraces to the cause of truth..., such course exposing the church to ridicule of her enemies, and cause the power of darkness to triumph.·[52]

·Avoid lawsuits if possible, for it gives Satan the advantage to entangle and perplex us. It is better to make settlement at some loss.·[53] ·The patient forbearance... is always the most conclusive argument.·[54] ·Love is unsuspecting, ever placing the most favorable construction upon the motives and acts of others. Love will never needlessly expose faults of other. It does not listen eagerly to unfavorable reports, but rather seeks to bring it to mind of one the defamed.·[55]

·By dwelling upon the fault of others, we change into the same image, but by bending to Jesus and taking His love and perfection of character, we become changed into His image.·[56] ·The strongest argument in favor of the Gospel is a loving and lovable Christian.·[57]

Think with US Attorney General Kelly Ayotte who said, ·Unfortunately, no matter how frivolous the lawsuit, you still, of course have to pay people to defend you on it.·

Have you been suing one another?

HOW TO AVOID LAWSUITS AGAINST ONE ANOTHER

- ❑ Write your complaint, read it many times, and then burn it.
- ❑ Forgive one another (Ephesians 4:32)
- ❑ Forgive one another so that your Father will forgive you (Matthew 6:14)
- ❑ Please the Lord, and He will make your enemies be at peace with you (Proverbs 16:7)
- ❑ Hold your peace; you will be counted as wise (Proverbs.17:28)
- ❑ Be a friend; love at all times (Proverbs 17:17)
- ❑ Endure all things (1Corinthians 13:7)
- ❑ Be a peacemaker (Matthew 5:9)
- ❑ Live peaceably with all men (Romans 12:18)
- ❑ Conquer all with love (Proverbs 10:12)
- ❑ Do not be boastful and arrogant (1Corinthians 13:4)
- ❑ Do not be quick to quarrel (Proverbs 20:3)
- ❑ Do not haste to court (Proverbs 25:8)
- ❑ Settle things quickly (Matthew 5:25)
- ❑ Reconcile (Luke 12:28)

PRAYER

Dear Heavenly Father, I confess that I am accusing ____________ about ________________. Help me, Father, to be more understanding and forgiving like You. At times, I have violated You but You never file charges against me, You only forgive, dear Father. I beg the Holy Spirit to guide my heart not to rush in filing charges against those who violated my rights. Give me a forgiving spirit in order to be at peace with others. This I pray in the name of Jesus Christ, my Lord and Savior. Amen.

AFFIRMATION

I am a child of Love, and I am a vessel of forgiveness. I will forgive not because I need to, but because it is the right thing to do, according to God's principle of love.

Politeness costs nothing but gains everything.

LADY MARY MONTLEY MONTAGU

He knows not when to be silent,
who knows not when to speak.

PUBLIUS SYRIUS

It is always a feast where love is,
and where love is, God is.

DOROTHY DAY

Marvin Marcelino

Wait For One Another

MEAL KILLERS

1. List down the negative things you observe during your family mealtime.

____

____

____

2. List down positive actions you will make in order to make your family mealtime be an avenue of love and happiness.

____

____

____

____

____

1. Why do we need to eat together as a family?

2. Give three disadvantages of a family spending mealtime together.

3. Give three advantages of a family spending mealtime together.

4. How should one behave during mealtime?

5. What atmosphere should be maintained at the table during mealtime?

Wait For One Another

When ye eat, wait for one another. 1 Corinthians 11.33 RSV

The dining table is set, check which of these scenes is similar with your family mealtime? Scene one. The father is hurrying up for work; the mother is rushing you to eat fast so you will not be late for school. Scene two. Everybody is silent at the table, for talking would be a mortal sin. Scene three. As the family starts eating, so does the quarrel. Scene four. As you start chewing your food, a parent is telling you how much your food costs. Scene five. After the last syllable of the call to eat, everybody rushes in and forgets all about saying the grace, and in minutes, they are gone. Scene six. You eat alone while everyone else is gone. Scene seven. You have such delicious food, but the mood is dry and lonesome. Scene eight. Everybody is present and eating but busy on each of their electronic devises. Scene nine. You have nothing but meager salt and rice, but the whole family is lovely and happy.

·When ye eat wait for one another· is a line written the background of the painting *The Lords Supper*, I once saw in my travels. I noticed that in Asian countries have similarities in mealtime culture; commonly to Asian people mealtime is a social function. To some, it is but a refueling of the physiological needs of the body.

Mealtime is socialization time, done at home, under the tree, by the river, in the park, or at the restaurant. Mealtime is a time when members of the family gather. It is a time when the family members have a good time.

However, times have changed, and it too changed

Marvin Marcelino

the good intention of mealtime. Today, many say that eating together as a family is not practical, especially in the fast urban life. Processed foods are preferred, than mother's best home recipe. Today, fast foods are in because of the trend change of lifestyle.

Mealtime is when we socialize with the members of our family. Parents just make sure that there is food left for the kids at home because that is all parents think kids need at mealtime. Mealtime is family time, which the family can enjoy, and the time when God sees how grateful your family is in receiving the blessings. Mealtime is when Jesus, the unseen visitor dines with your family.

Mealtime, though always done three times a day, should not become a burden but a joy. The meager food of noodles, rice, and soy sauce can turn into a gourmet feast. The reason is obvious a happy family around where all felt loved; respect is observed, pleasant talk maintained, and sharing is at its best.

What a family where mealtime is dashed with joy, sprinkled with comfort, sauced with contentment, served with warmth acceptance over the table cleansed of unchristian manners, where the invincible host God and the unseen visitor Jesus smiles. What a contrast it is to a home where there is sterling silverware, decorated dining table but no love. Angels cannot stay long in that home.

The family is a sacred circle. If one is missing, then it is not a family at all. Mealtime is a time for all the members of the family to meet together, to review the day, a time for delight, a time for praising, and a time when love, compassion, support, encouragement and prayer are felt and demonstrated.

During mealtime, avoid anything that will kill the person's appetite: no frowning, no finger pointing, no negative attitudes, and no arguments. Most of all mind your own table manners.

Spending a meal together in an atmosphere of

love is a sure sign of a happy family. It is the best time a child remembers, a time you are closer together. Mealtime is a symbol of love and happiness. Leo Tolstoy was right in saying, all happy family resembles one another, but each unhappy family is unhappy in its own way.·

·Let all things else, let parents surround their children with an atmosphere of cheerfulness, courtesy and love. A home where love dwells and where it is expressed in looks, in words, and in acts is a place where angels delight to manifest their presence.[58]

How is your family mealtime? Have you been waiting for each other?

Marvin Marcelino

HOW TO WAIT FOR ONE ANOTHER

- Get off with your busy schedule and activities.
- Set mealtime as a priority family time.
- Teach everyone a prayer of thanks and grace.
- Avoid scolding during mealtime.
- Avoid negative mood; that is contagious.
- Do not talk about business matters, just praises for each other.
- Do not frown at table.
- Do not quarrel.
- Do not shout, coerce, or force.
- Remember your table manners; say ·please·and ·thank you·
- Do not argue on who will wash the dishes; do it after the meal.
- Let everyone enjoy his ∕ her meal as if it were the last.
- Turn-off the TV or radio during mealtime.
- Absolutely no gadgets during mealtime.

PRAYER

Dear Heavenly Father, I admit I have shortcomings during family mealtimes. Teach me, Father, that every mealtime is family time and that You, dear God, and Jesus are the unseen visitors are present before our dining table. I beg the Holy Spirit to help me make our mealtime a blessing to every family member. This I pray in the name of Jesus Christ, my Lord and Savior. Amen.

AFFIRMATION

I am a channel of love and mealtime is a time when God the Father and Jesus and the Holy Spirit, the unseen visitors, dine with us. I will make it a point that our family mealtime is the best time for the family.

The size of man can be measured by the size
of the things that make him angry.
J Kenfield Morley

Anger is but one letter short of danger.
Dr. S. D. Hulse

Do Not Provoke One Another

DISPLEASERS

1. Write the things that easily provoke you to anger.

____

____

____

2. List down how you provoke others to anger.

____

____

____

____

____

3. Evaluate your answers from 1 and 2. Are they right? Are they fair?

1. Why do we provoke or displease one another?

2. Give three disadvantages of displeasing or provoking a person

3. Give three advantages of displeasing or provoking a person

4. How should a Christian face provocation?

5. How would you deal with a person who is fond of teasing another to anger?

Do Not Provoke One Another

Do not provoke one another. Galatians 5.26 RSV

A friend once asked Elizabeth Kenny, the famed Australian nurse and originator of the Kenny method of polio treatment, how she managed to stay constantly cheerful. A friend said, 'I supposed you were just born calmly and smiling.' 'Oh no!' laughed the nurse. 'As a girl, my temper often went out of bounds. But one day when I got angry at a friend over some trivial matters, my mother gave me the counsel that I have stored in my mind and have called upon for guidance ever since.' She said, 'Elizabeth, anyone who angers you conquers you.'[59]

Irascible people get angry quickly with the wrong people, for the wrong reason, and often at the wrong time and unlikely places. At times, they are too violent, but there is one good thing about them. they stop quickly.

To provoke means to cause to be angry, annoy, irate, vex, nettle, aggravate, exasperate, upset, enrage, or infuriate. Provocation comes as revenge, or a joke to try someone else's patience. Patience, on the other hand, is an intermediate state about anger. Anger can be provoked in many ways. Anger is good at the right time, at the right place, at the right reason, and at the right length of time as long as you do not sin (Ephesians 4.26).

The hyper-choleric are exceedingly quick tempered; they get angry at anything or at any occasion. The worst are the bitter people; they are hard to reconcile. They keep up their anger for long because they suppress their animosity, and their relief only comes in retaliation. Revenge provides them release of tension, and it can be for pleasure or pain.

A famous writer argued, 'Anger born of sensitive

Marvin Marcelino

morals is not sin. But those who are at any supposed provocation feel at liberty to indulge…, anger and resentment is the opening of the heart to Satan.[60] The Bible even forbids us to provoke one another because acts prompted by temper are rightly judged when unpremeditated. Moses was counted righteous because his anger was caused by provocation (Psalms 106:29, 30). Thus, we are not to provoke anyone, even our children, to anger (Colossians 3:21) or wrath (Ephesians 6:4).

Never provoke one even at the slightest degree of it against another. The spirit that is kept gentle when provoked will speak more effectively in favor of the truth than any argument however forcible.[61] There is power in silence; when impatient words are spoken to you, do not retaliate. Words spoken in reply to the one who is angry, usually act as a whip, lashing the temper to greater fury. But anger met by silence quickly dies away… resolving not to speak harsh, impatient words.[62]

Appeal to your heavenly Father to keep you from yielding to the temptation to speak in an impatient, harsh, willful manner to each other.[63] Love's agencies have wonderful power; they are divine. The soft answer, turns away wrath is the love that suffers long and is kind. The charity that covers a multitude of sin is the love one needs to learn.[64] John Tillotson noted, To be able to bear provocation is an argument of great reason, and to forgive it of a great mind.

Have you been provoking each other to anger?

HOW NOT TO PROVOKE TO ONE ANOTHER

- ❑ Be a peacemaker (Matthew 5:9)
- ❑ Remember that you are a royal priesthood (1Peter 2:9)
- ❑ Be kind (1Corinthians 13:4)
- ❑ Be patient (1Corinthians 13:4)
- ❑ Do not be arrogant (1Corithians 13:5)
- ❑ Endure all things (1Corinthians 13:7)
- ❑ Do not shout your answer (Psalms 15:1)
- ❑ Answer not a fool according to his folly (Proverbs 26:5)
- ❑ Do not repay evil for evil (Romans 12:17)
- ❑ Do not tease.
- ❑ Do not do provoke others to anger.
- ❑ Calm down.
- ❑ If you are angry, count one to a hundred before saying anything.
- ❑ If very angry, drink one to two glasses of water.
- ❑ If very mad, leave the place and take a cold shower.

PRAYER

Dear Heavenly Father, I confess that I have the habit of teasing, displeasing, and provoking ________________. Help me, Holy Father, to overcome this weakness. I beg the Holy Spirit to guard my heart from any hint of provocation or retaliation, provocation to hurt or to displease or annoy my neighbor. This I pray in the name of Jesus Christ, my Lord and Savior. Amen.

AFFIRMATION

I am a peacemaker, a child of God and I am not easily provoked to anger, because I am patient and longsuffering. I do not provoke or displease others because Christ gave His life for all and made us children of God.

Marvin Marcelino

What greater things for the two human souls…

to minister to each other in all sorrow,
share each other in all gladness.

GEORGE ELLIOT

Let the man who has and doesnt give,
break his neck and cease to live.

Let him who gives without a care,
gather rubies from the air.

JAMES STEPHEN

Minister To One Another

MISSING MINISTER

1.List names of people you have ministered to lately.

____

____

____

2. What does the Bible say about what to do as Christ's ministers? Read Matthew 25:35-46.

____

3.Rate yourself as a minister of Christ.

Faithful	10 9 8 7 6 5 4 3 2 1	Forgetful
Active	10 9 8 7 6 5 4 3 2 1	Idle
Responsible	10 9 8 7 6 5 4 3 2 1	Unconcern

CONFER. Guide questions for discussion

1. Do we really need to minister to one another? Explain.

2. What aspect of our life should not be included in ministering to another?

3. How can one minister to another?

4. Is ministering plainly the work of a church clergyman, or pastor?

5. To whom should we minister?

CONSIDER.

Marvin Marcelino

Minister To One Another

Did you know that you are a minister of God ₍2Corinthians 6.4₎? Everyone is a representative of Christ, and a minister of righteousness ₍2Corinthians 11.15, 23₎. We are laborers together with the heavenly angels in presenting Jesus to the world.[65]

Who made us competent to be ministers? Man have received gifts and being made a partner, in various graces of God ₍2Corinthians 3.6, 10₎.

In her book, *Ministry of Healing*, Ellen White wrote, ·All that profess to be children of God should bear in mind that, as ministers, you will be brought in contact with all classes of minds. These are the refined and the coarse, the humble and the proud, the religious and skeptical, the educated and the ignorant, the rich and the poor, these varied minds, cannot be treated alike yet all need kindness and sympathy. By mutual contact, our minds should receive polish and refinement. We are dependent with one another, closely bound together by the ties of human brotherhood.·

It is through *One Anothering* relationships that Christianity makes contact with the world. Every man and woman who has received divine illumination is to shed light on the dark pathway of those unacquainted with the right way. ·A relationship sanctified by the spirit of Christ must be improved in bringing souls to the Savior. Christ is not to be hidden away in the heart as coveted treasure, sacred and sweet to be enjoyed solely by the possessor.

We are to have Christ in us as a well of water, springing up into everlasting life, refreshing all who come in contact with us.[66]

To every minister, let him do as the ability God

has given him that all in good things be glorified through Jesus Christ. Charles Huddon Spurgeon, the great preacher is correct when he said, ·There are no crown bearers in heaven that were no cross bearers here below.· Paul's ministry is the best example we have in record (2Corinthians 6:3).

Here is a creed by E. E. Kaiser.

This is my creed. to do some good,

To bear the ills without complaining,
to press on as a brave man should.

For honors that are worth gaining
to do some service day by day.
in helping my toiling brothers.,

This is my creed to close my eyes,
to strive to be when each day dies.

Some better when the morning found me,
to keep my standards always high,
to find my task and always do it.
This is my creed - I wish that I
could learn to shape my action.

It is good to be a Christian and know it, but it is better to be a Christian and act it out. Note that God will never forget your labor and work of love (Hebrews 6:10). Great is the promises of God to those who minister (Isaiah 58:10, 11) Let this beautiful prayer of Reverend Robert Harold Schuller be our prayer also.

Lord, make my life a window for your light to shine through and a mirror to reflect Your love to all that I meet. Amen·

Have you been ministering to one another?

Marvin Marcelino

HOW TO MINISTER TO ONE ANOTHER

- ❑ Remember that you are called the Minister of God (Isaiah 61:6)
- ❑ Minister to the poor (Psalms 41:1-3)
- ❑ Be a minister of Christ (Romans 15:16)
- ❑ Open wide your heart (2Corinthians 6:13)
- ❑ Have confidence in Christ (2Corinthians 3:4)
- ❑ Let no fault be found in your ministry (2Corinthians 6:3)
- ❑ Be an example in words, in conversation, in charity, in spirit, in faith and in love (1Timothy 4:12)
- ❑ In every way, preach Christ (Philippians 1:18)
- ❑ Have the attitude of God (Psalms 72:12)
- ❑ Support the weak (Acts 20:35)
- ❑ Stand and minister in the name of the Lord (Deuteronomy 18:5)
- ❑ Minister to the poor, naked, and hungry (Matthew 25:44)
- ❑ Continue doing well, for this is our motto (Romans 2:7)

PRAYER

Dear Heavenly Father, I confess that I failed to minister to ________________. Teach me, Father, how to minister to other people. Jesus had ministered and had shown me how. I beg the Holy Spirit to guide me as I do my responsibility in ministering to my neighbors. This I pray in the name of Jesus Christ, my Lord and Savior. Amen.

AFFIRMATION

I am a minister of Christ and I have a responsibility to share the good news of salvation and to bring God's love to every heart. If I have loved strangers, blessed my enemies and drawn a heart closer to God today, then I have ministered.

Let go, why do cling to pain?
Why hold onto the very thing that which
keeps you from hope and love.

BHUDDIST PROVERBS

Hating people is like burning down
your house to get rid of a rat.

HARRY EMERSON FOSDICK

Grudge Not One Another

GROUCHY GRUDGER

1.   When I am reminded of a violation personally made against me, I ...____

Question and Answer

2.   Answer Yes or No
   a.   Do you swear occasionally because of a slight mistake?

   b.   Are you irritated when ignored?
   c.   Do you get mad when one is rude in commenting about your looks?
   d.   Do you regret saying terrible things to someone?
   e.   Do you complain about anything you see?
   f.   Do you feel bad when things do not fit your liking?
   g.   Do you feel good about yourself?
   h.   Do you keep your hurt feelings for a long time?
   i.   Are you fond of remembering all the faults done to you?

3.   Think about your grudging habit. Is it getting better, or is it getting worse?

CONFER. Guide questions for discussion

1.   Do we need to resent or harbor anger against another?

2.   Why should we not resent from one another?

3.   How long have you been harboring grudges against another?

4.   How do you confront a person who is fond of harboring grudges against another person?

5.   What would you do if you found your friend was harboring resentment against you?

6.   How would you remove a deep seated grudge?

Marvin Marcelino

Grudge Not One Another

Grudge not one another. James 5:9 KJV

One day, the devil felt particularly gratified that he was able to make a mirror that had an unusual quality of badly distorting anything it reflected. The nicest face became unbelievably ugly. The nicest landscape became like a very dry desert. When someone with a good thought smiled and looked at the mirror, the devil saw in it a grin or grimace.

The devil's followers were also delighted with their master's success. He turned the world upside down with it. So, he got the idea of flying back to heaven to make fun of the angels and even God himself with that mirror. The nearer he got to heaven, the more he grinned. His grin reflected so horribly in the mirror that it slipped from his hand, fell back to earth, and broke into thousand pieces. However, this caused even more trouble than before. For the mirror broke into pieces as fine as the grains of sand and blew about around the earth. Whenever a grain got into a person's eyes, it could not easily remove, and that the person thereafter always saw only the bad side, evil in things and people. The result is we hold grudges, and murmuring. This habit of seeing only the bad and evil is not natural in human; it comes from the devil.[67]

Grudging means having resentment, ill will, malice malevolence, pique, malignity, or something remembered wrong. Why do we grudge one another? We grudge and become indignant. It is anger and hate caused by a feeling of resentment and anger due to injury, insult, or maltreatment. These harbored ill feelings are remembered repeatedly, which causes conflicts.

When these ill feelings haunt us from time to time or when circumstance reminds us, it sparks anger and again toward the person who committed that mortal sin against you. This entices one again to imagine something painful to one's violator and prays that the wrath of heavens consumes them. Chuck Palaniuk noted, 'Nothing can hold a grudge for long enough to condemn its punishment. Nobody can hold a grudge that long, even God.'

Leo Buscaglia has lectured, 'Grudge never satisfies, nor heals. It keeps us from moving forward and starting again, it buries positive energies in negative actions, which serve only to exhaust and deplete us. It makes us suspicious and hesitant to trust again. It destroys our creativity and retards our growth.' Unresolved feelings of anger can affect your health; an unforgiving spirit can also result in provoking rashness and sin.[68] Henry George Burn said, 'Anger begins with folly and ends with repentance.' Surely, that happens all the time, is it?

A famous writer was right when she penned, 'Forbear reprimanding, and censuring, you are not adapted to reprove. Your words only wounds and sadden; they do not cure and reform. You should overcome the habit of picking at little things that you think are amiss. Be broad, generous, and charitable in your judgment of people and things. Open your heart to the light. Remember that duty has twin sister, love; these two when united can accomplish everything, but when separated, neither is capable of good.'[69]

'Love is unsuspecting, ever placing the most favorable construction upon the motives and acts of others. Love will never needlessly expose the faults of others.'[70] Examine your demands on others. Be open minded, remove any malice and suspicion on anyone. Decry complacency. Express your gratitude. Gladden you heart like a child. Give a soft answer. Manifest loyalty in words or deeds. Listen and apologize if you were wrong. Try to understand. Never envy anyone. Forgo grudges. Forgive your so-called enemies. Forgive yourself. Forgive others.

Give yourself a break from negative forces. Give your heart, mind, and soul to God. Take pleasure in the beauty of the earth. Think of someone who needs you and your help. Appreciate others with kindness and gentleness. Express only love. Siddhartha Gautama preached, ·The man who foolishly does me wrong, I will return it to him the protection of my most ungrudging love, and the worst evil come from him the more goodness shall go from me.· Is this not what Apostle Paul was telling us? Let us overcome evil with good ﹙Romans 12:21﹚ Remember, Aesop's reminder, ·People often grudge others what they cannot enjoy themselves.· Are you happy with the grudge you are keeping?

Have you been harboring hurt against one another?

HOW NOT TO HAVE GRUDGES TO ONE ANOTHER

- ❑ Be a minister of Christ (Romans15:16)
- ❑ Be a peacemaker (Matthew 5:9)
- ❑ Overcome evil with good (Romans 12:21)
- ❑ Do good to them that hurt you (Proverbs 25:21, 22)
- ❑ Forgive one another (Matthew 11:25)
- ❑ Bring every thought unto the obedience of Christ (2Corinthians 10:5)
- ❑ Bear the fruits of patience (Luke 8:15)
- ❑ Show meekness unto all men (Titus3:2)
- ❑ Be patient and kind (1Corinthians 13:4)
- ❑ Be humble in spirit (Matthew 5:5)
- ❑ Do not stir up anger; it can cause confusion (Proverbs 30:33)
- ❑ Do not hate; it causes separation (Proverbs 10:12)

PRAYER

Dear Heavenly Father, I admit that I have been harboring resentment, grudges, and anger against _______________.

Teach me, Father, to overcome this weakness by giving me a forgiving spirit. It has been here for a long time, and it keeps haunting me. It keeps me from being happy and creative. Jesus was nailed on the cross because of my sin, and He never held any grudge against me. I beg the Holy Spirit to guard my heart from any grudges against my neighbors. This I pray in the name of Jesus Christ, my Lord and Savior. Amen.

AFFIRMATION

I am a vessel of love and in me, there is no more place for grudges and resentment but only for forgiveness, joy and peace. I am filled with the spirit of patience and understanding.

My mind is only of pure thoughts, for I am a new creation in Christ.

One may smile and smile and be a villain.
WILLIAM SHAKESPEARE

I was a stranger, and you took me in.
JESUS CHRIST

Happy is the house that shelters a friend.
RALPH WALDO EMERSON

Practice Hospitality
To One Another

HOSPITABILITY TEST
Encircle the letter Y if your answer is yes and N for no.

1. Do you like people?   Y N
2. Do you appreciate visitors?   Y N
3. Do you feel good when people drop by your place?   Y N
4. Do you favor well-dressed visitors?   Y N
5. Do you regret having shared your last snacks?   Y N
6. Are you anxious about cleaning after the visitors?   Y N
7. Do you worry about what people say about your house? Y N
8. Do you find to be more comfortable when left alone?   Y N
9. Do you usually suggest another place than yours?   Y N
10. Do you like sharing?   YN

(If you have seven Yes then you are Hospitable)

1.   Why do we ought to be hospitable to one another?

2.   To what class of people should hospitality be offered?
     ☆ ☆ very poor   ☆ ☆ rich
     ☆ ☆ poor   ☆ ☆ very rich
     ☆ ☆ non-Christian   ☆ ☆ strangers
     ☆ ☆ Christian   ☆ ☆ very important people
     ☆ ☆ to all

3.   Give examples of how you can be hospitable to another.

Marvin Marcelino

4. How would you deal with those who are more hospitable
    to the church financier·than to the poor member of the
    church? Read James 2:1-7.

5. How should the rich and poor be treated according to the
    book of James (2:1-7)?

6. How do you deal with a person who grumbles after being
    hospitable?

Practice Hospitality
To One Another

*Practice hospitality ungrudgingly
to one another. 1 Peter 4:9 RSV*

A learned man came to town to test how hospitable a
hotel keeper was. He was told that the hotelkeeper gave
free meals to newcomers. Therefore, the wise man
dressed in ragged clothes and presented himself to the
designated hotel. But the manager was most unfriendly. He did
not even let the professor sit down. The professor left in
embarrassment.

The next day the professor bought a complete set of new
clothes and came back to the hotel. This time, the manager
greeted him with a deep bow and had him sit right next to him
at the table. He then ordered a meal of special delicacies. The
professor took his plate at the table, but he did not eat. Instead,
he kept dropping his food and drinks onto his new clothes. The
surprised manager asked what that was supposed to mean.
The guest answered, 'When I came in here yesterday in my old,
ragged clothes, you offered me nothing to eat. Today when I

arrived and well dressed, I must believe that this good meal is not meant for me but my nice clothes.[71]

Hospitality means conviviality, cordiality, friendliness, sociability, receptiveness, heartiness, and warmth. Hospitality is an act of being generous and kind, welcoming and entertaining guests and strangers.

While in Thailand, every time my ESL students from Taiwan come to class, they will ask me if I have eaten. I wondered and researched their culture. Interestingly, I found out that when they asked, 'Have you eaten?' they mean 'Am I doing my best to accommodate your presence.' A cultural trait that should be preserved and adapted by churches goers not the common greetings of lip service.

An author wrote, 'Love cannot long exist without expression. Let not the heart of one connected with you starve for the want of kindness and sympathy.[72] The book *Acts of the Apostles* by Ellen G White exhorts, 'Though he possess great faith would be worthless. He might display great liberality; but should he for some other motive than genuine love, bestow all his goods to feed the poor, the act would not commend him to the favor of God.[73]

When we offer hospitality, offer with love and genuine cordiality and without grudging. 'A Christian must have a sanctified tenderness and love, in which there is not impatience or fretfulness and rude or harsh manner must be softened by the grace of Christ.[74]

It is better not to entertain visitors if you regret having them mess up your house or eat your food. Where behind those smile masks the real feeling of selfishness that shows when you count every bite on the cookies you have served, run a rag after every step on the floor you polished well enough for your self-esteem, and swear not to have any stranger again to mess your house.

'Come out of the cold and stiff reserve. Give more love rather than exact it, cultivate cheerfulness. Let the sunshine into your heart, and it will shine upon those about you; be more sociable in your manners.[75] Selfish and cold formality have extinguished the fire of love, and dispelled the graces that should make fragrant the character.[76] A Sanskrit proverb said, "He who allows him his day to pass by without practicing generosity and enjoying life's pleasure is like a blacksmith's bellows – he breathes but does not live."

Ellen G. White reminds us that, "Far more than any sermon that can be preached is the influence of a true *hospitable* home upon human hearts and lives."[77] (italics mine)

Have you been hospitable to one another?

HOW TO BE HOSPITABLE TO ONE ANOTHER

- Be a minister of Christ (Romans 15:16)
- Have an open heart (2 Corinthians 6:13)
- Be an example to the believers in love (1 Timothy 4:12)
- Love others as you love yourself.
- Believe that they are also sons and daughters of God (1 John 5:2)
- Remember that God looks at the heart (1 Samuel 16:7)
- Avoid speculating (1 Timothy 4:7)
- Be hospitable to strangers; they may be angels (Hebrews 13:2)
- Do not be prejudiced against others' religion, status in life, color, or race.
- Cultivate an interest about other.
- Be receptive in words, facial expression, gestures, and eye contact.
- Treat strangers well (Leviticus 19:34)
- Be honest with yourself.

PRAYER

Dear Heavenly Father, I admit that I have not been hospitable towards _______________. Help me, Father, to open my house to visitors. Jesus was hospitable even to the undesirable. I beg the Holy Spirit to direct my heart away from selfishness and grumbling against my visitors. This I pray in the name of Jesus Christ, my Lord and Savior. Amen.

AFFIRMATION

I am hospitable; my heart is open as is my house. I will treat others as Jesus treats me.

Marvin Marcelino

Even if a unity of faith is not possible, a unity of love is.

HANS URS BALSTHASAR

Love is our true destiny. We do not find the meaning of life by ourselves alone - we find it with another.

THOMAS MERTON

We Belong To One Another

LONG TO BE
1. Scale your sense of belonging or being part of a group.

    I sense   10 9 8 7 6 5 4 3 2 1   I dont sense.

    I feel part   10 9 8 7 6 5 4 3 2 1   I feel left out

    ·Open and in· 10 9 8 7 6 5 4 3 2 1   Fitting in·

    Belong   10 9 8 7 6 5 4 3 2 1   Not Belong

2. Were you always trying to fit in·to feel you belong? If Yes, why? ____

____

3. What do you fear that others might see in you, that makes you think will be the basis to exclude you in among them?

____

____

1. Do we really need a group to belong to?

2. Name the risks one will have to take to belong. ₍vulnerability, rejection, expectations, etc..₎

3. How does it feel to be left out·, rejected by a group, or told that you lack something to belong to their group. Share.

4. Give examples of advantages and disadvantages belonging to a group.

5. How would you deal with those who ·segregate·themselves

Marvin Marcelino

from others? Read Matthew 12:25.

6. How should each other be treated according to 1 Corinthians 1:10?

We Belong To One Another

*So we, being many, are one body in Christ,
and individually members of one another. Romans 12:5 NRSV*

There was this story of a bat who tries to fit in·in a group of animals. There was a division among the birds and the mammals. One day there was suspicion among each group about a suspected spy who is a member of both groups. The leader of the birds went through all bird and interrogated each. Until the bat was asked, you seem to be different?·The leader of the birds said. ᐸ belong with you, you see, I fly, like everybody else here. Animal cant fly like us⌁, the bat replied. The leader of the birds, Okay you may stay but we will bring matter to the Supreme Council.·On the other camp, the animals have had their council and interviewed each animal, until it went with the bat. Wait a minute said the leader of the animals. You seem so peculiar. Are you one among us?· The bat said, ᐸ am one among you, sire. Look I have fur, sharp fangs, pointed ears, looks like a mean animal.·And the leader of the animal said, We will bring your case to the Supreme Council.·

All the animals gathered quietly to hear the verdict of the Supreme Council. The head of the Supreme Council said, The bat was created just as unique as everybody. You are all created uniquely from each other. If you are all created the same wouldn't life be boring? Why do you have to put up fly·and non-flying·or feathered·and furred·classification amongst you. The same reason I did not make each the same. I want you to learn to accept each other and learned to live together in this world. From now on let no animals or birds say something about this dear bat. Go and show the humans that you animal kingdom can belong together.·And all the birds and the animal

Marvin Marcelino

accepted the bat and made him feel it belongs to both groups just as he was created, and everybody lived peacefully.

We all wanted to be part of something significant because this adds value to our being. Just knowing that we are not alone gives us courage, strength and hope that there are people who will back you up in life, let alone being accepted and loved. That is the sense of belonging. Belonging is being accepted just as you are, you without trying to fit in· or feeling like you must behave like this and that or do this or that just to feel important as a member of a company. A close family gives each of its members a strong sense of belonging without condition and expectations. William R. Bradford puts it picturesquely, ·Within each of us there is an intense need to feel that we belong. This feeling of unity and togetherness comes through the warmth of a smile, a handshake, or a hug, through laughter and unspoken demonstrations of love. It comes in the quiet, reverent moments of soft conversation and in listening.·

The futility of world leaders running after peace in the world now, Mother Teresa saw what was missing, she said, ·If we have no peace, it is because we have forgotten that we belong to each other.· Brené Brown adds, ·A deep sense of love and belonging is an irreducible need of all people. We are biologically, cognitively, physically, and spiritually wired to love, to be loved, and to belong. When those needs are not met, we do not function as we were meant to. We break. We fall apart. We numb. We ache. We hurt others. We get sick.·

·It is God's purpose to manifest through His people the principles of His kingdom *which is love*. That in life and character they may reveal these principles, He desires to separate them from the customs, habits, and practices of the world *which cultivates envy, jealousy, and hate*. He seeks to bring them near to Himself that He may make known to them His will *which is love and that we may cling to it because it is where we belong*. ·italics mine)·T6.p91)

When the grace of God reigns in the heart, there is purity, freedom from sin. The glory, the completeness, the fullness of the Gospel plan is fulfilled in the life. When self is submerged in Christ, true love springs forth spontaneously. The impulse to help and bless others springs constantly from within. Toil for others' good is not regarded as drudgery. It is a cheerful work, done with a glad heart. Sympathy with Christ, participation in His joy, sweetens all toil. It braces the will. It nerves the spirit for whatever may befall. The soul is surrounded with an atmosphere of faith and courage and Christ-like love, an atmosphere invigorating to the spiritual life of all who inhale it. (AUSCR July 1, 1900)

Through love you were created, through love you were born and only in Love you belong. Martin Luther King Jr. once preached, ·Darkness cannot drive out darkness only light can do that; Hate cannot drive out hate only LOVE can do that.·

It is a joyous experience to have to belong to something where love reigns. For this matter to be part of the One anothering family in Christ Jesus.·

If you are with us in spreading love to one another, William Arthur Ward is reminding us to, ·Do more than belong, participate. Do more than care. help. Do more than believe, practice. Do more than be fair. be kind. Do more than forgive, forget. Do more than dream. work.·

Have you made clear to others that both of you belong to one another in love?

HOW TO BELONG TO ONE ANOTHER

- ❑ To belong is to be in Spirit and to have the Spirit (Jude 1.19)
- ❑ Be a minister of Christ (Romans15.16)
- ❑ Have an open heart (2Corinthians 6.13)
- ❑ Be an example to the believers in love (1Timothy 4.12)
- ❑ Love others as you love yourself. (John 13.34)
- ❑ Believe that we all are sons and daughters of God (1John 5.2)
- ❑ Remember that God looks at the heart (1Samuel 16.7)
- ❑ Avoid speculating (1Timothy 4.7)
- ❑ Let there be no divisions among you (1 Corinthians 1.10)
- ❑ Let there be no distinctions among you (Galatians 3.28)
- ❑ Be of one mind with Christ and the Father. (John 17.21)
- ❑ Treat strangers equally well (Philippians 23.4)
- ❑ Be part of any fold, whose Shepherd is Christ Jesus (John 10.16)

PRAYER

Dear Heavenly Father, I admit that I draw an invisible line between us and them. Help me, Father, to open my mind and heart attract people to desire to belong to Christ Jesus. I beg the Holy Spirit to direct my heart away from the spirit of segregation and discrimination against other people of God. This I pray in the name of Jesus Christ, my Lord and Savior. Amen.

AFFIRMATION

I belong to Christ Jesus the only true Shepherd. I will see others as part of Jesus' other folds and all of us belong to God.

When man is a partaker of the divine nature,
the love of Christ will be an abiding principle
in the soul, and self will not be exhibited.

ELLEN G. WHITE

The heart benevolent and kind
the most resembles God.

ROBERT BURNS

Love One Another, The Way Jesus Did

BRANCHED VINE

What loving qualities does Jesus have that I too possess?

JESUS   ME

_________________   _________________
_________________   _________________
_________________   _________________
_________________   _________________
_________________   _________________
_________________   _________________

CONFER. Guide questions for discussion

1. Is it possible for us to love one another like the way Jesus loved each of us?

2. What would hinder us from loving one another like Jesus did?

3. If everyone will love like the way Jesus did, what would you think would happen? (In our homes, church, community and world)

4. Would the kind of Love Jesus showed us solve the conflict around us?

5. How would you teach a person who does not know how to love like Jesus did?

Love One Another,
The Way Jesus Did

Love one another as I have loved you. John 15.13 RSV

rene Sharp wrote a beautiful prayer. Today, Lord is every day of my life. Give me ears that hear my brother's cry, eyes that see my brother's needs, feet that stand beside him, hands that heal and feed and above all, a heart overflowing with love.

The command, Love one another as I have loved you may seem impossible to do - but if one trust and believe, great are the joys that one will receive. Remember that love is a power that transforms the world. Love not only the few dear to you, but love all - the publican, the sinners, and the legalists. Practice love for we have a Great Teacher who taught us how to love.

How did Christ manifest his love for the poor mortals? He sacrificed His glory, riches, and life for us. Christ consented to a life of humiliation and great suffering. He submitted to the cruel mocking of infuriated and murderous multitude, and to the agonizing death upon the cross.[78]

Those who follow Christ's example of self-denial for the truth's sake make a great impression on the world. Their example is convincing and contagious. Men see God's people who work in love and purify their souls from selfishness.

A new commandment I gave unto you that ye love one another as I have loved you that ye also love one another. To the disciple this is a new commandment for they had not loved one another as Christ has loved them. He saw

Marvin Marcelino

that new idea and impulses must control them; they must practice the new principles; through his life and death, they were to receive a new concept of love.

The command to ·love one another· has a new meaning in the light of self-sacrifice. ·The whole work of grace is the one continual service of self-denying self-sacrificing effort.·[79] ·He desires only the service of love; love cannot be commanded, and it cannot be won by force or authority. Only love begets love.·[80] ·He who claims to abide in Christ should give daily evidence that he is emulating his Savior.·[81]

No matter how high his profession, he whose heart is empty of love for God and his fellow men is not a true disciple of Christ. This love is evidence of their discipleship. ·By this shall all men know that ye are my disciples,· said Jesus. ·When men are bound together, not by force or self-interest, but by love, they show the working of an influence that is above every human influence.[82]

·Love for the lost soul brought Christ to Calvary's cross.·[83] ·Christ bound men to His heart by the ties of love and devotion, and by the same ties, He bound them to their fellow men. With Him, love was life and life were service.[84] ·Jesus did not live for himself…, He is constantly ministering for others…His whole life was under a law of service. He serves all, ministered to all…, he lived the law of God and by His example showed how to obey it.·[85]

·Who can comprehend the love of Jesus? If we know the value of the human soul, we must look in living faith upon the cross, and thus begin the study, which shall be the science and the song of the redeemed through all eternity. The value of our time and our talent can be estimated by the greatness of the ransom paid for our redemption.·[86]

Dante wrote, ·The love of God, unutterable and perfect, flows into a pure soul the way light rushes into a transparent object. The more love he receives, the more love shines forth; so that· as we grow clear and open, the more complete joy of loving is. And the more souls who resonate together; the greater intensity of their love for, mirror like, each soul reflects the other.·

Have you loved one another with the kind of love Jesus showed you?

HOW TO LOVE ONE ANOTHER LIKE JESUS DID

- ❑ Love the children of God ₍1John 5.2₎
- ❑ Love those who love God ₍1John 4.21₎
- ❑ Let brotherly love continue ₍Hebrews 13.1₎
- ❑ Walk in Love, as Christ has loved us ₍Ephesians 5.2₎
- ❑ Know the love of Christ ₍Ephesians 3.19₎
- ❑ By love, serve one another ₍Galatians 5.3₎
- ❑ Prove the sincerity of your love ₍2Corinthians 8.8₎
- ❑ He that loves another fulfills the commandment ₍Romans 13.10₎
- ❑ Work no ill ₍Romans 13.10₎
- ❑ Do justly love mercy ₍Micah 6.8₎
- ❑ Honor thy father and thy mother ₍Exodus 20.12₎
- ❑ Do not kill ₍Exodus 20.13₎
- ❑ Do not steal ₍Exodus 20.15₎
- ❑ Do not bear false witness ₍Exodus 20.16₎
- ❑ Do not covet ₍Exodus 20.17₎

PRAYER

Dear Heavenly Father, I confess that have not loved ________________ the way Jesus loved me. Help me, Father, to learn the way Jesus loves. He even sacrificed His life for my sake. I beg the Holy Spirit to guide my heart to offer my love and life to another. This I pray in the name of Jesus Christ, my Lord and Savior. Amen.

AFFIRMATION

I am a loving person like Jesus. I am ready to sacrifice, for I am a true follower of Christ and a living testament of the Truth and of Love.

In love is all the law we need,
In Christ is all the God we know.

EDWIN MARKHAM

To know and not to do,
is not yet to know.

BHUDDIST PROVERBS

Loving One Another, Fulfills The Law

LAW ABIDING CITIZEN

1. What significant lessons from this book have affected and challenged you to change the way you love one another?

__________________ __________________
__________________ __________________
__________________ __________________
__________________ __________________

2. What lessons from this book are hard to follow?

__________________ __________________
__________________ __________________
__________________ __________________
__________________ __________________

CONFER. Guide questions for discussion

1. Are you able to love *Agape*?

2. Is Jesus the center of your love?

3. Are you having a hard time following God's law?

4. How do you see yourself after reading and understanding this chapter?

5. Can people now feel the power of love within you?
    ⭐ ⭐ If YES - go affect and infect others
    ⭐ ⭐ If NO - go read this book again

Loving One Another, Fulfills The Law

...he that loveth one another hath fulfilled the law. Romans 13:10 RSV

Have you experienced driving? While enjoying the drive, an officer suddenly stops you and gives you a ticket for not knowing how to drive. Fined, and ordered you to attend a seminar on ·Driving 101.· You wondered after being a driver for many years; ask yourself, ·What lack you?·

God's Traffic Rules

John the Beloved wrote, ·And by this we may be sure that we know him if we keep his commandments. He who says I know Him· but disobeys His commandments is a liar and the truth is not in him, but the love of God is perfected truly in him whosoever keep his words. By this, we may be sure that we are in him: he who says he abides in Him ought to walk in the same way in, which He walked. ·(1John 2:3-6)

Helen Steiner Rice, the Ambassador of Sunshine wrote, ·Blessed are they that walk in love, for they walk with God above.· The follower of Christ will give evidence of the transforming power of the Holy Spirit in the daily life, justice, mercy and love of God will be seen.·[87]

We are to reflect the highest attribute of the character of God. We should be thankful to know that we are never left to ourselves. The law of God is to be exalted standard to which we are to attain through the imputed righteousness of Christ.·[88] ·Unless you accept in your own life the principles of self-sacrificing love, which is the principle of His character, you cannot know God.·[89] ·It is the greatest and most fatal deception

to suppose that a man can have faith unto life eternal,

162

without possessing Christ-like love for his brethren.[90]

Are You Controlled by The Love of God?

Paul has prepared an answer for that inquiry, God's love which has been given to us through the Holy Spirit has been poured into our hearts (Romans 5:5). This love is not impulse but diverse principles, a permanent power. The unconsecrated heart cannot originate it or produce it. Only in the heart where Jesus reigns it is found. We love him because He first loved us.

In the heart renewed by the divine grace, love is the ruling principle of action. It modifies the character, governs the impulses, controls the soul, sweetens the life and shed the refining influence on all around.[91]

We may be active, we may do so much work; but without love, such love as dwelt in the heart of Christ, we can never be numbered with the family of God in heaven.[92] There is not an iota (dot) of the love of God while hatred is cherished in the soul.[93]

No matter how many qualities we may have, however honorable and refined we may consider ourselves if the soul is not baptized with the heavenly grace of love of God and one another. We are deficient in the true goodness and unfit for heaven, where all is love and unity.[94]

When Christ dwells in the heart, the soul is filled with His love, with the joy of communion with Him that it will cleave to Him; and in the contemplation of Himself will be forgotten. Love to Christ will be the spring in action. A profession of Christ without this deep love is mere talk, dry formality and heavy drudgery.[95]

God's law is the love He has surrounded you with beauty to teach you that you are not placed on earth merely to; delve for self, to dig and built, or to toil and spin. You can make life bright and joyous and beautiful with the love of Christ, like the flowers to gladden other lives by the ministry of love.[96]

Knowledge of what God has done for us awakens love. Love motivates obedience. When God's love becomes the focus of our lives, it becomes apparent in obedience to his laws and in our love for others.[97]

Have you been trying to fulfill the law of God without loving (agape) one another?

HOW TO LOVE ONE ANOTHER
AND FULFILL THE LAW

- ❏ Keep yourself in the love of God (Jude 21)
- ❏ Love one another because this is the trademark of Christ's disciples (John 13:35)
- ❏ Love your neighbor (1John 4:21)
- ❏ Be compelled by the love of God (2Corinthians 5:14)
- ❏ Know the love of Christ (Ephesians 3:19)
- ❏ Abide in love (1John 4:16)
- ❏ Love the children of God (1John 5:2)
- ❏ Love those who love God (1John 4:21)
- ❏ Let brotherly love continue (Hebrews 13:1)
- ❏ Walk in Love, as Christ has loved us (Ephesians 5:2)
- ❏ Know the love of Christ (Ephesians 3:19)
- ❏ By love, serve one another (Galatians 5:3)
- ❏ Prove the sincerity of your love (2Corinthians 8:8)
- ❏ Loves another and fulfill the commandment (Romans 13:10)
- ❏ Remember that love works no evil (Romans 13:10)
- ❏ Love your brother (1John 4:20)
- ❏ Remember, many hold the form of religion but deny the power of it (2Timothy 3:5)

PRAYER

Dear Heavenly Father, I confess that I have not loved ________________ the way a Christian should. God the Father and Jesus have loved me, though I sometimes followed the law but did not love. At times, I have loved but faked it and I have not followed God's law. Help me, Father, to learn the ways of the heavenly love. I beg the Holy Spirit to guide my heart that I might sincerely love my neighbor so I can fulfill the law of God. This I pray in the name of Jesus Christ, my Lord and Savior. Amen.

AFFIRMATION

I will love others according to the commandments of God. By loving another I will fulfill God's laws, and others will know that I am a true disciple of Christ Jesus.

I sought my soul, but my soul I could not see.
I sought my God, but my God eluded me.
I sought my brother, and I found all three.
AUTHOR UNKNOWN

If we do not show love to one another,
the world has the right to question
whether Christianity is true.
FRANCIS A. SCHAEFFER

If We Love One Another, God Lives in Us

CONFRONT.

YOU ARE GOD'S RESIDENCE

1. Can God reside in you? ☆ ☆ Yes   ☆ ☆ No

   Why?

   ____

2. If YES, what positive characteristics you think you possess?

   ____________________   ____________________

   ____________________   ____________________

3. If NO, What negative behavior do you have that hinders God from residing in you?

   ____________________   ____________________

   ____________________   ____________________

CONFER. Guide questions for discussion

1. Have you loved one another? If Yes, how did you do it? If No, why did you not?

2. When can we say that God lives in us? How will that happen?

3. Why is God's love in the heart more important than keeping the law?

4. How do you see yourself now after reading this chapter? How do you rate yourself? (1 Lowest and 10 Highest)

5. Can the people around you feel the presence of God within you?

If yes, share how to do. If no, explain.

If We Love One Another, God Lives in Us

*...but if we love one another, God lives in us
and His love is made complete in us. 1John 4:12 KJV*

One day, an old man sat down by a deep well, gave himself a grateful drink, and looked down the well. A curious little boy came and tried to pull himself up to the rim of the well to have a look. The old man laughingly scooped the boy into his arm and pointed to the well. 'Do you know who lives down there?' He asked. The boy replied, 'No.' 'God lives down there. "Look,"the old man said. The boy stared down into the well, and all he could see was his own reflection. 'Thats me.' The boy excitedly said. 'Ah,' the man replied, 'Now you know where God lives.'

Did you know that God is in you? How are you to know that God is in your heart? Apostle Paul said, 'Examine yourself, to see if you are abiding by your faith. Test yourselves, unless indeed you fail to meet the test'(2Corinthians 13.5). Everyone in whose heart Christ abides, everyone who will show forth his love to the world is a worker together with God for the blessings of humanity.'[98]

'What each one needs is the Christ in the heart, because when self merges in Christ, love springs forth spontaneously.'[99] When Christ dwells in the heart, His presence is apparent. Good and pleasant words and action reveal the spirit of Christ where it manifests sweetness of temper. There is no angry passion, no obstinacy, no evil surmising, and there is no hatred in the heart.'[100]

If we abide in Christ, the love of God dwells in us, then our feelings, our thoughts, our purposes, and our actions will be in harmony with the will of God as expressed in the

169

precepts of His holy law.[101] ·It is by beholding His love, by dwelling upon it, by drinking it in that we are partakers of his nature.·[102]

·Abiding in Christ means a constant receiving of His spirit as the vine branch constantly draws the sap from the Living Vine so are we to cling to Jesus, and receive from Him faith the strength and perfection of His own character.·[103]

·You just cant hide whats inside you. ·The love of Christ binds together the members of the family, and whenever that love is manifested, it reveals the divine relationship.·[104]

A young helper was beginning her first day in the hospital ward. She was nervous. She could see the dying men lying on the beds. She saw the other helpers moving from bed to bed, pouring water here. giving kind words there, touching hands, and giving medicine.

Suddenly, Mother Theresa came to her and said smiling, ·Sister come to me. I want you to meet someone.· The young helper followed Mother Theresa. Soon, they arrived at a bed in the far corner of the ward. On the bed lay a human skeleton. His eyes had sunk deep into his head. His hair was gone. He only had one tooth.

Mother Theresa took the old mans head in her hands and knelt by the bed. ·Sister Anna,· she said to the young helper, ·I want you to meet Jesus.·[105]

As the hymn says, ·Can the world see Jesus in you? Can the world see Jesus in me? Does our light come shining through; can the world see Jesus in us?

·The greatest thing a man can do for his heavenly Father,· said Henry Drummond, ·is to be kind to His other children.·

Do you want God to be in your midst? Then love one another. As this poem *GOD IS LOVE* says by yours truly.

> *If you do not love,*
> *you do not know God.*
>
> *If you hate to love,*
> *you hate God.*
>
> *If you do not care to love,*
> *you do not care about God.*
>
> *But if you look at others through love,*
> *you will see and know God.*
>
> *So why the need to love?*

Marvin Marcelino

HOW TO HAVE GOD LIVE WITH US

- ❑ Do the will of God from the heart (Ephesians 6:6)
- ❑ Keep yourself in the Love of God (Jude 21)
- ❑ Love the children of God (1John 5:2)
- ❑ Love those who love God (1John 4:21)
- ❑ Live peaceably with all men (Romans 12:18)
- ❑ Live according to God's spirit (1Peter 4:6)
- ❑ Live honestly (Hebrews 13:18)
- ❑ Let Christ live in you (Galatians 2:20)
- ❑ Live by the power of God (2Corinthians 13:4)
- ❑ Live godly in Christ Jesus (2Timothy 3:12)
- ❑ Live soberly and righteously and godly (Titus 2:12)
- ❑ Live in the spirit (Galatians 5:25)
- ❑ Come close to God, and God will be close to you (Jas 4:8)
- ❑ Remember that your body is God's temple (1Cor. 6:19)
- ❑ Follow the entire How to·in this book.

PRAYER

Dear Heavenly Father, I admit that I have not made my body ready for God to reside. I know that my body is the temple of God and at times, I have denied the power the Spirit gave me. Help me, Father, to learn the ways of the heavenly love. I beg the Holy Spirit to guide my heart that I will love my neighbor and cleanse my soul, so that this body becomes a dwelling place of God. This I pray in the name of Jesus Christ, my Lord and Savior. Amen.

AFFIRMATION

I am God's creation. My body is a temple, a residence of the Holy God and I am to keep this body clean by advocating love to one another. Then I will know that God is in me.

Living the life of faith is not always glorious
or dramatic; it is mostly mundane;
it is done day by day in little act of love.

JOHN S. NIXON

To love for the sake of being loved is human,
but to love for the sake of loving is angelic.

ALPHONSE DE LAMARTINE

Sincerely Love One Another From The Heart

SINCERELY YOURS

1. Can you **sincerely** love one another? ☆ ☆ Yes ☆ ☆ No

2. If yes, how?

   ____

3. If no, when?

   ____

CONFER. Guide questions for discussion

1. What hinders one from loving another?

2. When is a person sincere in his or her love (agape) to another?

3. What qualities must human possess to be sincere in loving?

4. Do you understand the reason/s of your existence?

5. Are you following God's law?

6. What do you think of the reward of the faithful? Is it fair?

Sincerely Love One Another From The Heart

...love one another deeply from the heart. 1Peter 1.22 NIV

The Truth

God is love. If one lives in love, one lives in God and God in him. Love makes each of us complete so that we can stand confidently on the Day of Judgment (1John 4.16) (v. 7)

For us to understand love, God sent his only begotten Son Jesus as a sacrifice for our sins, (v.10) - sin like being uncaring to one another.

You did not choose this, but God chose you (John 15.16) because you are a royal priesthood and a chosen generation (1Peter 2.9) Therefore, prepare your mind for action (**One Anothering**); be self-controlled and loving; set hope fully on the grace to be given you when Christ Jesus is revealed in you.

As obedient children of God do not conform to the evil desires as you did when you lived in ignorance. Just as He who called you is holy, be also holy in all you do, for it is written, be holy because I Am holy (1Peter 1.13-16) Jesus said, You are no longer of this world anymore (John 17.14, 16) If anyone loves the way of the world, the love of the Father is not in him (1John 2.15, 16)

The Law

God is a God of order. A reason why there is a need of laws or commandments. That is if one turns his back to God, he will meet God's laws, but if he focuses on God, His laws will be behind him. If we love God, then we will keep His commandments, not for His good but our own sake (John 14.15)

The law of God is perfect and good to those who follow it. (James 1:25) FF Bruce, in his book *The Epistle of John*, wrote, "Love is the supreme manifestation of the new life, so much so that anyone who fails to manifest it that he has never entered into the new life, he still abides in death."[106]

Follow David's attitude, "Oh, how I love your law! I meditate on it all day long; your commands make me wiser than my enemies" (Psalm 119:97) "Search me, O God and know my heart; test me and know my anxious thoughts. See if there is any offense in me and lead me in the way everlasting" (Psalm 139:23, 24).

The Task

Our task is to love, the main reason why we exist. First, we ought to love God. "Love the Lord your God and walk in His ways with all your minds, with all you souls, and with all your heart" (Matthew 22:37, 38) By doing so, we will be able to let other people understand the mysteries of God; His commandments; the plan of salvation and what Christ Jesus died for. Love is never without a reason, and it is not blind, it sees what the eyes cannot. It is pure and holy; pure love will take God into its entire plan and will in perfect harmony with the spirit of God.[107]

Second, we ought to love one another. When we say we love God but hate our brothers, we are counted liars (1John 4:19) It is stated in the law that if we love God, we also love other people (v. 20, 21) **One Anothering** may seem hard to do only because we have not been used to it. Loving is not how one forgive, but how one forgoes the hurt. Loving is not how good one discipline, but how well one let the offender understand the principles of God. Loving is not how well one expose the wrong of others, but how one understands why they do it. Loving then are leading others to God.

Loving is how one free oneself from grudges, pain, and the

unpleasant memories of the past. Loving is how one let go and free yourself from being a slave to hatred, anger, and bitterness. Loving is how one endure malice, criticism, prejudices, injustice, persecution and condemnation through patience and long-suffering. Jesus took this path, and He won. Loving is when one is terribly been hurt and can no longer take another hurt and is almost ready to give in, but then he realize that he love the offenders more.

Loving is not how much one have given, but how sincerely it was shared. Loving is not about how many people saw one doing good deeds to others, rather it is measured by how God sees one doing it for His glory. Loving is not how much one have gained, but how much more one want to lose. Loving is not whom one thinks he is, but how ready one want to be what God wants one to be.

Loving is not for one to be loved, admired, accepted or to be praised when one is not. Loving is being honest to self, to others and most of all, to God. Loving is admiring the undeserving, but not consenting to evil deeds. Loving is not too strict that it distorts the ideals of God and godliness. Loving is not setting oneself as the standard; loving is being blameless in the sight of God. The Psalmist says, Blessed are they whose ways are blameless who walk according to the law of the Lord (Psalm 119:1). God's grace is sufficient for us (2Corinthians 12:9). We have faith, hope and love, but love is the greatest of these (1Corinthians 13:13).

The Reward

The highest motive of a Christian is not to live the better life to acquire certain rewards, though these properly have their place, but rather to live a better life in recognition of the fact that in and of itself, it is a better life. A Christian finds ultimate satisfaction in living harmony with the great eternal principles of the Kingdom of heaven.[108] God wants each of us to find His place, and when each one is in his place, doing the work that God has given him, there will be perfect harmony.[109] ·The ultimate lesson for us to learn,· said Elizabeth Kubler Ross, is that unconditional love, not only to others, but to ourselves as well. ·

Yes, practicing **One Anothering** has its reward. Jesus promised us that when He comes back, he will bring with Him our reward ᵣRevelation 22:12₎ Jesus will reward us according to our deeds ₍Jeremiah 17:10₎ The faithless will be fully repaid for their ways, and the good man rewarded for his ᵣProverbs 14:14₎

The ultimate reward is that where God is, where Jesus is, there we will also be, in a place prepared for us ₍John 14:1-3₎

Through purifying yourselves by obeying the Truth, you will have sincere love for one another deeply from the heart.

For you have been born again not by perishable seed, but by imperishable seed, through living and enduring word of God ₍1Peter 1:22-23₎

Go and do **One Anothering**.

HOW TO SINCERELY LOVE ONE ANOTHER

- ☐ Live honestly (Hebrews 13:18)
- ☐ Let Christ live in you (Galatians 2:20)
- ☐ Live by the power of God (2Corinthians 13:4)
- ☐ Live godly in Christ Jesus (2Timothy 3:12)
- ☐ Live soberly and righteously and godly (Titus 2:12)
- ☐ Live in the spirit (Galatians 5:25)
- ☐ Do the will of God from the heart (Ephesians 6:6)
- ☐ Keep yourself in the Love of God (Jude 21)
- ☐ Love the children of God (1John 5:2)
- ☐ Love those who love God (1John 4:21)
- ☐ Live peaceably with all men (Romans 12:18)
- ☐ Live according to God's spirit (1Peter 4:6)
- ☐ Come close to God and God will be close to you (James 4:8)
- ☐ Do not imitate evil, do what is good (3John 11)

PRAYER

Dear Heavenly Father, I admit that at times I am not sincere in loving other people. Help me, Father, to learn the way you sincerely loved me. Jesus has shown how sincere He was when He gave His life for me at the cross. I beg the Holy Spirit to purify my heart that I will sincerely love my neighbor. This I pray in the name of Jesus Christ, my Lord and Savior. Amen.

AFFIRMATION

I am sincere. My love to my neighbor is pure and blameless. However, trials pass me; my sincere love to my neighbor is enough because God's grace is sufficient for me.

We have just enough religion
to hate but not enough to
make us love one another.

JONATHAN SWIFT

The opposite of love is not hate,
Its apathy.

LEO BUSCAGLIA

Love is not only something you feel.
It's something you do.

DAVID WILKERSON

Overcoming Proclivity

ONE ANOTHERING AUDIT

Check from the list of Biblical principles of Love you have applied in your life.

- ☐ Doing What I Hate to Do
- ☐ The Rule of Psychological Reciprocity
- ☐ The Basics of Interpersonal Relations
- ☐ 180 Degrees Metamorphosis
- ☐ Be Devoted To One Another
- ☐ Advise One Another
- ☐ Offer Humility To One Another
- ☐ Accept One Another
- ☐ Admonish One Another
- ☐ Activate One Another
- ☐ Encourage One Another
- ☐ Instruct One Another
- ☐ Greet One Another
- ☐ Live In Harmony With One Another
- ☐ Continue Having Debt of Love To One Another
- ☐ Serve One Another
- ☐ Be Kind and Compassionate With One Another
- ☐ Build One Another
- ☐ Speak To One Another
- ☐ Submit To One Another
- ☐ Bear One Anther
- ☐ Forgive One Another
- ☐ Slander Not One Another
- ☐ Devise No Evil To One Another
- ☐ Speak the Truth To One Another
- ☐ Love One Another
  - ☐ Forbear One Another

- ☐ Fellowship With One Another
- ☐ Exhort One Another
- ☐ Carry One Another's Burden

- ☐ Speak the Truth To One Another
- ☐ Confess Your Sin To One Another
- ☐ Pray For One Another
- ☐ Wash One Another's Feet

- ☐ Comfort One Another
- ☐ Honor One Another
- ☐ Do Not Destroy One Another
- ☐ Execute Justice To One Another
- ☐ Envy Not One Another
- ☐ Judge Not One Another
- ☐ Grumble Not One To Another
- ☐ Care For One Another
- ☐ Do Not Refuse One Another
- ☐ Be At Peace With One Another
- ☐ Do Not Lie To One Another
- ☐ Have No Lawsuits Against One Another
- ☐ Wait For One Another
- ☐ Do Not Provoke One Another
- ☐ Minister To One Another
- ☐ Grudge Not One Another
- ☐ Practice Hospitality To One Another
- ☐ We Belong to One Another
- ☐ Love One Another Like How Jesus Loved
- ☐ Loving One Another Fulfills the Law
- ☐ If We Love One Another God Dwells In Us
- ☐ Sincerely Love One Another By Heart
- ☐ Overcoming Proclivity

1.   Has this book blessed you? If Yes, how? If No, why?

2.   Are you ready to share the principles you have learned?

3.   What principles are you hard up to follow?

4.   How do you see yourself now after reading this book?
     How do you rate yourself? (1 Lowest and 10 Highest)

5.   Can you say that you are now a loving person?
     If Yes, Explain how did you do it?
     If No, Explain when or how would you do it.?

CONSIDER.

Overcoming Proclivity

Keep in the love of God. Jude 21 NIV

desired and dreamed to ride a bicycle. I must be able to drive a bicycle. I told myself. Though it seems impossible for some reasons, I do not have a bicycle and yet not allowed play rough outside so how can I learn how to bike. We are poor enough to afford a bike, which made me decide to forget all about riding a bike because it seems impossible to come true, but the urge of determination tells me to find a way.

I waited for the opportunity to ride a real bike. I waited, and imagined while waiting, mentally picture that I was riding a bike. In my mind, I practiced. Yes, I was only dreaming that I am riding a bike.   It took a long time, seems all wishing, and dreaming are failing because events do not cooperate with my prayers. Most of the time all circumstances disappoint me, but my determination is sure.

One day it happened; there was a bike, but it was not mine, my neighbor had a new bicycle. I cannot wait to try it for myself. I waited for the opportunity but, while waiting, I mentally prepared myself to ride a bike. The day I had been waiting came when my neighbor friend called me to try his new bicycle. The chance I have been waiting for has come. Mentally and theoretically, I know how to ride a bike, and I was so excited and drove as if I know how to ride a bike. I literally do not know the basics like how to balance, to pedal and steer.

Euphoric and just rode and drove the new bicycle for the first time, the next thing is I was on the ground. I got up with all the dirt over me, and scratches on my knees and elbows, my first day on the bike was a failure. Always thinking I will fail, and never will be able to ride a bike again, but consistent in my mind is the determination to ride a bike because I love doing it, even though the probabilities to err, to fail and hurt myself is high; I never gave up.

My friend did not blame me for the scratches on his new bike. He even encouraged me to try again, and he taught me how. Wished I had more that day, but it was time to go home. My small dream came true. Days came I improved some more, and the more I progress, the enjoyable biking is.

However, at times I fall or went straight to a garbage pit, accidentally run over a dog, fall flat on a ground, and go down in a canal. Those experiences did not stop me from enjoying my biking. The unpleasant experiences gain me knowledge on how to avoid errors on biking. The secret: I was determined to do the right way.

I took that experience because it has similarities with loving. Loving one another is like learning to ride a bike. Many times, you fail and almost to give up. Failing to love may be like the first day you ride a bike as if failures is saying you will never learn how to love. In loving, proclivity is evident and present, but one can avoid and overcome it.

Everybody wants loved.

Each one desires to love and be loved, most of us are wishing this dream to happen. Yes, many tried silly ways from fancy clothes to personal gadgets, to materialism just to attract somebody to love you. Reading between the lines, we are telling another that what you have are valuable, and therefore, saying, ‘I am valuable too.’

We do extra ordinary things to be accepted starting from extra ordinary talents to extreme games to get the attention, we long from significant others. We strive to be on top from political position, to academics, to materialism, and to stardom. We crave for attention because being on top brainwashes us to believe that nothing is more important but self. We are saying, ‘Look I can do this, now tell me that I am good. If you do, I will feel good then I know that you love me, and I have your attention, too.’

Lovely, lovable, loving but lost, that is who we are and how lost are we? Both the urge to love and being loved lingers and never ceases. Like my desperate dream to ride a bike, but we ride anything from stick broom to mop and tree branches, but never the real bike. The hunger and craving never stop and we enjoy riding the floor mop. We tried to quench the pangs of loneliness that grip each of us in the midst of many loved ones. Our naturalization to be more unloving increases in this deceitful world. This makes us more feel unloved, and self-centered, rather than God and other centered.

We tried to be lovely, to be loveable and to being loving. Yet we are afraid to come out to the open for fear of failure, for fear of disappointment, for fear of discouragement, for fear of ridicule, and of being ignored again. Our fear has left us stuck inside our wishes and dreams.

At times, this emotional longing drives one erroneously to seek through the needs of the flesh. The lingering thought that when another skin kisses another skin, it is believed to be love. We thought skin-to-skin love or flesh-to-flesh gives one warm and security, but usually two empty and lost human beings seeking to love and be loved. The more we seek by our own flesh the more each sink in the quagmire of their loneliness.

It is never harmful to love *(agape)* one another. Sadly, we live in the haven of the seven deadly sins, which are envy, lust, greed, gluttony, anger, hatred, and selfishness. We grew here, and blindly accept what appears to be nothing we can do about, and the more we become indifferent. When the cycle of apathy becomes unusually intense, more people drift from each other, and the more one gets lost in the presence of many, a total stranger in the company of one's own family.

One Anothering is a call to wake up from the trance of indifference. You are a creation in the image of a loving God and loving you must be. Wake up to the new Way! Wake up to the reality of Life! Wake up to the Truth! Jesus is the Way the Truth and the Life (John 14:6) There is a place I know a place where one can go to learn how to be loving!

Church School for One Anothering

Howard Clinbell, author of *Pastoral Care Counseling* wrote that the purpose of the church is to improve the quality of life for the member rather than remaining self-centered. Clinebell has broadened the view of the good life that we normally considered. He wrote saying that a Christian congregation should accomplish, *The mission of the church is to be abundant life center, a place for liberating, nurturing and empowering life in all it fullness, to individuals an intimate relationship.*

Let us have a minute theological study on the

word 'church' in its original meaning; it does not refer to a building or structure. The Greek word *ekklesia* means a group of people taken out of the darkness of sin and into the glorious light (1Peter 2.5, 9)

God's grace is pulling us out of the darkness from the sins of indifferences, of selfishness, of being uncaring, and of being unlovable. Therefore, we are being liberated or freed from self-centeredness. The purpose of the Church is to nurture us in love, to empower us in love, and that each of us may grow in faith and unto good works. We now love one another because God first loved us (1John 4.9) We serve one another through Jesus (Mark 10.45) We love as created (Matthew 28.18-20) Then the people of this world will know that we who love one another are God's witnesses (John 17.21)

The Church is not a place for righteous people only. Nobody is righteous not even one (Romans 3.10) Jesus came not for the saints but for the sinners, the unlovable, the unloving (Matthew 9.12, 13) Therefore, do not expect the Church to be in perfect state. That perhaps tells us why all sorts of interpersonal and behavioral conflicts and *whaddyamaycallit* problems exists. No, not yet many church members are good only on the church doctrines but loving one another seems to be a new idea to them. Give them allowance to learn how to love. Allow them to adjust and practice perfectly **One Anothering**.

The Church is greatly deficient of love. Some are reserve cold, chilling; it preserved an irony of dignity that repels those who brings within their influence. The spirit is contagious; it creates an atmosphere that is withering the good impulses. It chokes the natural current of human sympathy, cordiality and love; under its influence people become constrained and their social and generous attributes are destroyed for want of exercise.[110]

Do you know that the church is still the best place on

earth? Homes are broken beyond repair. Schools have gone wayward that focuses more on success and material acquisitions. Governments are prisoners of their own corrupt system. So where else could we run? I know one. Yes, we still have one refuge in God (Psalms 46:1), God has a chosen people, and one among them is you (John 15:16) So, return to your home and declare what God has done for you (Luke 8:9)

W. Somerset Maugham noted, ·The tragedy of love isn't death, the tragedy is indifference.·It is love alone can solve the human conflicts and problems. Do not limit yourself. Seth, a writer said, ·Self is not limited.· Make this a point in life as William James asserts that, ·I will act as if what I do make the difference.·That difference is through *One Anothering*

This book did not present a new concept. God has formulated the idea in the beginning of everything. God the Son, Christ Jesus exemplified the concept in His life on earth. Jesus uttered this *One Anothering* concept many times, ·Love one another.·

If you think you cannot love, here is a Dayak proverb ·Where the heart is willing it will find a thousand ways, but where it is unwilling it will find a thousand excuses.· Ask yourself this· Is it truly YOU CANNOT, or YOU WON·T?

Try *One Anothering*, I know, you can· As Ralph Waldo Emerson said, ·They can conquer who believe they can.· I say, ·They love who believes they can·

Go ahead LOVE·

HOW TO OVERCOME PROCLIVITY

- ❑ Live honestly (Hebrews 13:18)
- ❑ Let Christ live in you (Galatians 2:20)
- ❑ Live by the power of God (2Corinthians 13:4)
- ❑ Live godly in Christ Jesus (2Timothy 3:12)
- ❑ Live soberly and righteously and godly (Titus 2:12)
- ❑ Live in the spirit (Galatians 5:25)
- ❑ Do the will of God from the heart (Ephesians 6:6)
- ❑ Keep yourself in the Love of God (Jude 21)
- ❑ Love the children of God (1John 5:2)
- ❑ Love those who love God (1John 4:21)
- ❑ Live peaceably with all men (Romans 12:18)
- ❑ Live according to God's spirit (1Peter 4:6)
- ❑ Come close to God and God will be close to you (James 4:8)
- ❑ Lack of love destroys life (1John 3:12)
- ❑ If I have not love, I am nothing (1Corinthians 13:2)

PRAYER

Dear Heavenly Father, I confess that I still have the strong tendencies to do the wrong at times. Help me Father to overcome these tendencies of being unloving. I beg the Holy Spirit to direct my heart to do the right and the proper way to love this I pray in the name of Jesus Christ, my Lord and Savior, Amen.

AFFIRMATION

I am purified. I am now a new creation. I am lovely. I am loveable and I am more loving. By God's grace and mercies, I will be part of the heavenly family of Love.

Nobody can do it for you.
RALPH CORDINER

No one will do it for you.
BEN STEIN

You have to make it happen.
JOE GREENE

What Are You Waiting For
Go Love One Another

Check which reason is stalling you to love

☆ ☆ I cant start, I need help

☆ ☆ I do not know how to start, I need a guide

☆ ☆ I am scared to try

☆ ☆ My guilt is holding me back

☆ ☆ I need forgiveness from people I have hurt

What Are You Waiting For
Go Love One Another

Do what it says. James 1:22 NIV

There is no perfect time in doing *One Anothering*. There is only today and now. I urge you to begin your journey to greater level of better interpersonal relationship. Do not wait until everything is just right, it will never be perfect in these last days. Dorothy Day suggest that ·We must lay one brick at a time, take one step at a time; we can be responsible only for the action of the present moment. But we can pray for an increase of Love in our hearts that will vitalize and transform all our individual actions.·

There will be obstacles, hardships, and impossibilities; there will be trials, disappointments, discouragement, trials, and persecution. then so what. Get started now! Each step you take, makes you grow more and more stronger, more and more understanding, more and more caring, more and more and more loving. David Lloyd George is right, Dont be afraid to take a big step. You cant cross a bog chasm in two small jumps.·

The challenge is waiting for us to apply *One Anothering*. There is no new concept introduced. The same principles Jesus told and showed is the same we need to do to one another. Dorothy Parker simply illustrates that Love is like a quicksilver in the hand. Leave the fingers open and it stays. Clutch it, and it darts away.·

GO, do not dream, start slowly, and build up and love. Friedrich Nietzche said, He who would learn to fly one day must learn first to stand and walk and run and climb and dance; we cannot without trying.·As an adage urge us that the only way to start is to start, the first step is the hardest.· Confucius knew this, that ”a journey of thousand miles begins with one step.· What moves a man said Antoine de Saint Exupery is to take a step then another.·

Ralph Cordiner is right, nobody can do it for you.·So is Ben Stein, No one will do it for you and Joe Greene supports that, you have to make it happen.· William Faulkner is inspiring to say, the man who removes a mountain begins by carrying away small stones.·

I hope vou have enjoyed through the principles of *One Anothering*. I hope that you have more awareness about the importance of better interpersonal relationship.

Every person you meet or relate with is a potential recipient of love and all you must do is apply *One Anothering*. Do not wait for the day to come when the risk to remain tight in a bud was more painful than the risk to blossom. Novalis Hardenberg has this in closing, Love is the final end of the worlds history, the Amen of the universe.·

Thank you for sharing these pages with me. My prayer for you is that you love, love and love until all will love each other than heaven will never be a fiction.

PRAYER

Dear Heavenly Father,
Grant us the true love for one another,
That we may be a part of those whom you have chosen and loved,
Even to all the unbelievers whom Christ died for.

Help us to understand each other, to be more patient and kind,
That as we grow in love we become closer to each other.

Heavenly Father,
You are a God of Love
You know how much it takes to suffer, to pain and remain in Love.

Allow us to perfect this love especially for our dear ones,
Reminds us that without You, our love to one another can never be perfect.

Heavenly Father,
Share us the fullness of Your love the perfection of Your character.

Plant in our hearts Your lovely nature of redemptive grace and mercy,
That when two strange soul meet they response to one another with Love,
Then a little heaven of eternal glory is experienced
Amen.

AFFIRMATION

Today, I will love my neighbor for tomorrow maybe too late. God's grace and mercies will usher me through. I will not allow this day to pass without applying *One Anothering.*

Marvin Marcelino

AND THE GREATEST OF THEM ALL IS LOVE

Marvin A. Marcelino

No greater philosophy can ever outwit the wisdom of love.

No greater religion ever existed but the religion of Love.

No greater belief has ever been proven tacit than love.

No greater doctrine can ever replace the precepts of love.

No greater commission was given to mankind but to love God and man.

No greater duty is nobler for man to do but to love his neighbor.

No greater education can be taught than the experience of loving.

No greater extreme challenge exists than loving those who hurt and hate you.

No greater security can ever be reliable than being surrounded by love.

No greater economic crisis could bring to poverty a loving person.

No greater joy can ever be felt than the result of loving the unlovable.

No greater hope one could cherish than finding out somebody loves you.

No greater experience can one have but to love and be loved.

No greater technology can ever teach the manners Love.

No greater opportunity one could grab than the elusive moment to love.

No greater reward could match any grand prize than the consolation of love.

No greater sin is ever unpardonable by a merciful and forgiving Love.
No greater dream anybody ever aspire than to be truly loved.
No greater punishment is effective to any stubbornness but a firm love.
No greater psychological treatment could ever relieve the mind but Love.
No greater ugliness exists when viewed through the mirror of love.
No greater heroic deed can ever surpass the simple acts of love.
No greater cold apathy can ever divide us from the warmth of love.
No greater distance can ever be far that love could not reach.
No greater heights are ever too high that love could not touch.
No greater government is ever stable than the one whose foundation is love.
No greater nation can ever be stronger than a people who love each other.
No greater wealth of the entire world combined can ever buy a priceless Love.
No greater death is ever sweet than to die in the name of Love.
No greater language can ever be universal than the language of love.
No greater force can ever be stronger than the strength of love.
No greater war is ever fought than the battle of Love against sin and hate.

No greater evil is ever wicked that was not defeated

by the power of Love.

No greater deity that has ever existed than the God that is Love.

No greater of all the greatest in the whole universe but Love.

Yes, and the greatest of all is LOVE.

I Have a Request

have a request: I want you to write and tell me how this book has affected your life. Share me your stories and adventure with **One Anothering**.

Let me know how you have made a difference as a result of reading this book. What new secrets have you discovered in relating to one another? What tips do you have that I can pass on to the future generations?

Do you have a favorite story, quote, and an insight about **One Anothering**? *(Biblical Guide to a Christian Interpersonal Relations)*

Please send it to me I am eager to hear from you. Thank you for participating in one another's life.

Please e-mail me at the following address.

Marvin A. Marcelino

at
marvzmarcelino@gmail.com

About the Author

Marvin A. Marcelino is a graduate of Bachelor of Art in History and Philosophy of Religion and Bachelor of Theology at Adventist University of the Philippines.

He served an instructor in a Philippine government leadership institution.

He taught Values subjects in colleges and secondary Christian schools for some time. He is presently working in an international school in Bangkok, Thailand.

He is a frequent speaker to many youth and family camps, retreats, fellowships, seminars and conferences. He is always invited as resource person in the Philippines, Thailand, Malaysia, and Vietnam.

He is a coach, mentor, a trainer, a guidance counselor, a facilitator, a teacher, a father and a friend to many young and adult.

He conducts seminars and training on leadership, management, human relations and youth and family matters.

He enjoys creating, values-oriented activities for the youth.

His other interests include reading, writing, filmmaking, photography, digital arts, swimming, painting, hiking, biking and camping.

He is married to Jasmin Jimenez Marcelino a registered dietician. They were blest with three children, Joshua Marvin and Mayumi Jasmine and Mark Jiro.

He has written several books,

Marvin Marcelino

References

1. Ellen G. White, *Testimonies to the Church Vol. 8*, (Mountain View, CA. Pacific Press Publishing Association, 1948), p. 240.

2. __________, *Ye Shall Receive Power*, (Hagerstown, MD. Review and Herald Publishing Association, 1995), p. 121.

3. Frank F. Mihalic, *1000 Stories You Can Use, Vol. 1*, (Manila. Divine Word Publication Inc., 1989),

4. Ellen G White, *Gospel Workers*, (Washington D.C. Review and Herald Publishing Association, 1948), p.120.

5. Ellen G. White, *The Review and Herald*, May 31, 1892, par. 6.

6. *Seventh Day Adventist Bible Commentary Vol. 3*, (Washington D.C. Review and Herald Publishing Association, 1978) p. 1164.

7. Ellen G. White, Reflecting *Christ*, (Hagerstown, MD. Review and Herald Publishing Association, 1985), p.234.

8. Frank F. Mihalic, *1000 Stories You Can Use, Vol. 1*, (Manila. Divine Word Publication Inc., 1989), p.223.

9. Ellen G. White, *Christ Object Lessons*, (Washington D.C. Review and Herald Publishing Association, 1900), p. 144.

10. __________, *The Great Controversy Between Christ and Satan*. (Mountain View, CA. Pacific Press Publishing Association, 1907), p. 620.

11. Ellen G. White, *Testimonies to the Church Vol. 4*, (Mountain View, CA. Pacific Press Publishing Association, 1948), p. 169

12. Frank F. Mihalic, *1000 Stories You Can Use, Vol. 2,* (Manila: Divine Word Publication Inc., 1989), p. 139.

13. Ellen G. White, *Christ Object Lessons,* (Washington D.C.: Review and Herald Publishing Association, 1941), p. 143.

14. Frank F. Mihalic, *1000 Stories You Can Use, Vol. 2,* (Manila: Divine Word Publication Inc., 1989)

15. Ellen G. White, *Evangelism,* (Mountain View, CA.: Pacific Press Publishing Association, 1911), p. 275.

16. Frank F. Mihalic, *1000 Stories You Can Use, Vol. 1,* (Manila: Divine Word Publication Inc., 1989)

17. James A. Tucker and Priscilla Tucker, *Glimpse of Gods Love,* (Washington D.C.: Review and Herald Publishing Association, 1883), p. 25.

18. Frank F. Mihalic, *1000 Stories You Can Use, Vol. 2,* (Manila: Divine Word Publication Inc., 1989),

19. Ellen G. White, *Our High Calling,* (Washington D.C.: Review and Herald Publishing Association, 1961), p. 180.

20. __________, *Testimonies to the Church Vol. 4,* (Mountain View, CA.: Pacific Press Publishing Association, 1948), p. 348.

21. *The Seventh-day Adventist Bible Commentary.* Ellen G. White *Comments. Vol.* 6 (Washington, D.C.: Review and Herald Publishing Association, 1970), p. 1111.

Marvin Marcelino

22. __________, *Sons and Daughters of God*, ₍Washington D.C. Review and Herald Publishing Association, 1995₎, p. 185.

23. __________, *Ministry of Healing*, ₍Washington D.C. Review and Herald Publishing Association, 1905₎, p.187.

24. __________, *God's Amazing Grace*, ₍Washington, D.C. Review and Herald Publishing Association, 1973₎, p. 256.

25. __________, *Testimonies to the Church Vol. 5*, ₍Mountain View, CA. Pacific Press Publishing Association, 1948₎, p. 606.

26. __________, *Patriarchs and Prophets*, ₍Silver Spring, MD. General Conference Ministerial Association, 1995₎, p. 308.

27. Frank F. Mihalic, *1000 Stories You Can Use, Vol. 1*, ₍Manila. Divine Word Publication Inc., 1989₎, p. 47.

28. *The Seventh-day Adventist Bible Commentary. Ellen G. White Comments. Vol. 7* ₍Washington, D.C. Review and Herald Publishing Association, 1970₎, p. 1157.

29. .Ellen G. White, *Testimonies to the Church Vol. 5*, ₍Mountain View, CA. Pacific Press Publishing Association, 1948₎, p. 124.

30. Ellen G. White, *Testimonies to the Church Vol. 3*, ₍Mountain View, CA. Pacific Press Publishing Association, 1948₎, p. 547.

31. Frank F. Mihalic, *1000 Stories You Can Use, Vol. 2*, ₍Manila. Divine Word Publication Inc., 1989₎, p. 135.

32. Ellen G. White, *The Masters Immortal Sermons*, (Mountain View, CA. Pacific Press Publishing Association, 1971), p. 15.

33. Frank F. Mihalic, *1000 Stories You Can Use, Vol. 1*, (Manila. Divine Word Publication Inc., 1989), p. 177.

34. Ellen G. White, *Desire of Ages*, (Mountain View, CA. Pacific Press Publishing Association, 1940), p. 650.

35. Ibid., p. 310.

36. *The Seventh-day Adventist Bible Commentary. Ellen G. White Comments. Vol. 3* (Washington, D.C. Review and Herald Publishing Association, 1970), p. 1163.

37. __________, *Selected Messages. Vol. 2*, (Washington D.C. Review and Herald Publishing Association, 1958), p. 71.

38. __________, *Testimonies to the Church Vol. 2*, (Mountain View, CA. Pacific Press Publishing Association, 1948), p. 116.

39. __________, *Testimonies to the Church Vol. 7*, (Mountain View, CA. Pacific Press Publishing Association, 1948), p. 183.

40. Frank F. Mihalic, *1000 Stories You Can Use, Vol. 2*, (Manila. Divine Word Publication Inc., 1989),

41. Ellen G. White, *Sons and Daughters of God*, (Washington D.C. Review and Herald Publishing Association, 1995), p.83.

42. __________, *Testimonies to the Church Vol. 6*, (Mountain View, CA. Pacific Press Publishing Association, 1948), p. 283

43. Frank F. Mihalic, *1000 Stories You Can Use, Vol. 2*, (Manila. Divine Word Publication Inc., 1989), p. 194.

44. Ibid., p. 194

45. Ellen G. White, *Testimonies to the Church Vol. 4*, (Mountain View, CA. Pacific Press Publishing Association, 1948), p. 64.

46. Frank F. Mihalic, *1000 Stories You Can Use, Vol. 2*, (Manila. Divine Word Publication Inc., 1989)

47. Ellen G. White, *Testimonies to the Church Vol. 5*, (Mountain View, CA. Pacific Press Publishing Association, 1948), p. 565.

48. __________, *Spiritual Gifts. Vol. 4.* (Battle Creek, MI. Seventh day Adventist Publishing Association, 1960), p. 43.

49. __________, *Child Guidance*, (Washington D.C. Review and Herald Publishing Association, 1958), p.150.

50. __________, *Child Guidance*, (Washington D.C. Review and Herald Publishing Association, 1958), p. 388.

51. __________, *Child Guidance*, (Washington D.C. Review and Herald Publishing Association, 1958), p. 152.

52. __________, *Testimonies to the Church Vol. 5*, (Mountain View, CA. Pacific Press Publishing Association, 1948), p. 242.

53. __________, *Testimonies to the Church Vol. 1*, (Mountain View, CA. Pacific Press Publishing Association, 1948), p. 202.

54. __________, *Ministry of Healing*, (Washington D.C. Review and Herald Publishing Association, 1905), p. 494.

55. __________, *Testimonies to the Church Vol. 5*, (Mountain View, CA. Pacific Press Publishing Association, 1948), p. 168.

56. __________, *Gospel Workers*, (Washington D.C. Review and Herald Publishing Association, 1948), p.479.

57. __________, *Ministry of Healing*, (Washington D.C. Review and Herald Publishing Association, 1905), p. 470.

58. __________, *Ministry of Healing*, (Washington D.C. Review and Herald Publishing Association, 1905), p. 387.

59. Frank F. Mihalic, *1000 Stories You Can Use, Vol. 2*, (Manila. Divine Word Publication Inc., 1989), p. 98.

60. Ellen G. White, *Desire of Ages*, (Mountain View, CA. Pacific Press Publishing Association, 1940), p. 310.

61. __________, *Reflecting Christ*, (Hagerstown, MD. Review and Herald Publishing Association, 1985), p.293.

62. __________, *Messages to Young People*, (Nashville, Tennessee. Southern Publishing Association, 1950), p. 136.

63. __________, *Adventist Home*, (Nashville, Tennessee. Southern Publishing Association, 1952), p. 342.

64. __________, *Adventist Home*, (Nashville, Tennessee. Southern Publishing Association, 1952), p. 195.

65. __________, *Desire of Ages*, (Mountain View, CA. Pacific Press Publishing Association, 1940), p. 297.

66. __________, *Testimonies to the Church Vol. 4*, (Mountain View, CA. Pacific Press Publishing Association, 1948), p. 555.

67. Frank F. Mihalic, *1000 Stories You Can Use, Vol. 2*, (Manila: Divine Word Publication Inc., 1989), p. 43.

68.

69.
70.
71.
72.
73. Ellen G. White, *Testimonies to the Church Vol.5*, (Mountain View, CA. Pacific Press Publishing Association, 1948), p.501.

74. __________, *Testimonies to the Church Vol.4*, (Mountain View, CA. Pacific Press Publishing Association, 1948), p.62

75. __________, *Testimonies to the Church Vol. 5*, (Mountain View, CA. Pacific Press Publishing Association, 1948), p. 168.

76. Frank F. Mihalic, *1000 Stories You Can Use, Vol. 2*, (Manila: Divine Word Publication Inc., 1989), p. 236.

77. Ellen G. White, *Ministry of Healing*, (Washington D.C. Review and Herald Publishing Association, 1905), p. 360.

78. __________, *Testimonies to the Church Vol. 5*, (Mountain View, CA. Pacific Press Publishing Association, 1948), p. 168.

79. __________, *Testimonies to the Church Vol. 5*, (Mountain View, CA. Pacific Press Publishing Association, 1948), p. 335.

80. __________, *Testimonies to the Church Vol. 4*, (Mountain View, CA: Pacific Press Publishing Association, 1948), p. 104.

81. __________, *Desire of Ages*, (Mountain View, CA: Pacific Press Publishing Association, 1940), p. 504.

82. __________, *The Faith I Live By*, (Washington, D.C.: Review and Herald Publishing Association, 1958), p. 278.

83. __________, *Testimonies to the Church Vol. 1*, (Mountain View, CA: Pacific Press Publishing Association, 1948), p. 690.

84. __________, *God's Amazing Grace*, (Washington, D.C.: Review and Herald Publishing Association, 1973), p. 145.

85. __________, *Desire of Ages*, (Mountain View, CA: Pacific Press Publishing Association, 1940), p. 22.

86. __________, *Ye Shall Receive Power*, (Hagerstown, MD: Review and Herald Publishing Association, 1995), p. 121.

87. __________, *Lift Him Up*, (Mountain View, CA: Pacific Press Publishing Association, 1988), p. 293.

88. __________, *The Faith I Live By*, (Washington, D.C.: Review and Herald Publishing Association, 1958), p. 309.

89. __________, *Education*, (Mountain View, CA: Pacific Press Publishing Association, 1952), p. 80.

90. __________, *Desire of Ages*, (Mountain View, CA: Pacific Press Publishing Association, 1940), p. 106.

91. __________, *The Sanctified Life*, ⸤Washington, D.C.⸥ Review and Herald Publishing Association, 1956⸥ p. 93.

92. __________, *Desire of Ages*, ⸤Mountain View, CA⸥ Pacific Press Publishing Association, 1940⸥, p. 107.

93. __________, *Our High Calling*, ⸤Washington D.C.⸥ Review and Herald Publishing Association, 1961⸥, p. 364.

94. __________, *Maranatha; The Lord Is Coming*, ⸤Washington, D.C.⸥ Review and Herald Publishing Association, 1976.⸥, p. 88.

95. *The Seventh-day Adventist Bible Commentary.* Ellen G. White Comments. Vol. 5 ⸤Washington, D.C.⸥ Review and Herald Publishing Association, 1970⸥, p. 1141.

96. __________, *Reflecting Christ*, ⸤Hagerstown, MD⸥ Review and Herald Publishing Association, 1985⸥, p.234.

97. __________, *Christ Object Lessons*, ⸤Washington D.C.⸥ Review and Herald Publishing Association, 1900⸥, p. 158.

98. __________, *Our High Calling*, ⸤Washington D.C.⸥ Review and Herald Publishing Association, 1961⸥, p. 158.

99. __________, *Testimonies to the Church Vol.4*, ⸤Mountain View, CA⸥ Pacific Press Publishing Association, 1948⸥, p. 223-224.

100.__________, *Steps to Christ*, ⸤Mountain View, CA⸥ Pacific Press Publishing Association, 1956⸥ p. 44-45.

101.__________, *Lift Him Up*, ⸤Mountain View, CA⸥ Pacific Press Publishing Association, 1988⸥, p.73.

102.__________, *Selected Messages*, (Washington D.C.: Review and Herald Publishing Association, 1941), p. 337.

103.__________, *Testimonies to the Church Vol. 2*, (Mountain View, CA: Pacific Press Publishing Association, 1948), p. 227.

104.__________, *Christ Object Lessons*, (Washington D.C.: Review and Herald Publishing Association, 1900), p. 384.

105.__________, *This Day with God*, (Mountain View, CA: Pacific Press Publishing Association, 1979), p. 357.

106.__________, *Steps To Christ*, (Mountain View, CA: Pacific Press Publishing Association, 1952), p. 61.

107.__________, *My Life Today*, (Mountain View, CA: Pacific Press Publishing Association, 1952), p. 275.

108.__________, *Desire of Ages*, (Mountain View, CA: Pacific Press Publishing Association, 1952), p.676

109.__________, *Gods Amazing Grace*, (Mountain View, CA: Pacific Press Publishing Association, 1952), p.52

110.Frank F. Mihalic, *1000 Stories You Can Use, Vol. 2*, (Manila: Divine Word Publication Inc., 1989)

111.Bruce. FF, *The Epistle of John*, (London: Pickering and Inglis, 1970), p. 95.96.

112.__________, *The Adventist Home*, (Mountain View, CA: Pacific Press Publishing Association, 1952), p. 51.

113.__________, *Testimonies to the Church Vol. 2*, (Mountain View, CA. Pacific Press Publishing Association, 1948), p. 233.

114.__________, The *Upward Look*, (Washington, D.C. Review and Herald Publishing Association, 1982), p. 157.

115.__________, *Testimonies to the Church Vol. 4*, (Mountain View, CA. Pacific Press Publishing Association, 1948), p. 63.

Bibliography

1. Beattie, Melody., *Codependent No More.* Minnesota Hazelden Foundation, 1992.

2. Buscaglia, Leo., *Living, Loving and Learning.* New York Ballantine Books Inc., 1985.

3. __________. *Loving Each Other.* New Jersey. Slack Inc., 1984.

4. Cabbab Juliet and Cabbab, Mark Anthony., *Speech Com Manual,* Manila Bookmark, 1984.

5. de Chavez, Delba. *Learning is Fun So Is Teaching.* San Pablo City, 1999.

6. Davidoff, Henry., ed. *The Pocket Book of Quotations.* N.Y. Pocket Books, Simon Schuster Inc., 1994.

7. De Ville, Jard., *The Pastors Handbook on Interpersonal Relationships.* Maryland. Review and Herald Graphics, 1995.

8. *Familiar Quotations.* Ottenheimer Publisher Inc., 1962; reprint ed., Caloocan City. National Bookstore, 1970.

9. Gothard, Bill. *Institue of Basic Youth Conflicts.* USA. n p., 1981.

10. Mihalic, Frank F., *500 Stories You Can Use.* Manila. Divine Word Publication Inc., 1993.

11. __________. *1000 Stories You Can Use, Vol. 1 and 2.* Manila. Divine Word Publication Inc., 1989.

Marvin Marcelino

12. Morgan, J. S. and Philp, J. R. , *You cant Manage Alone.* Michigan.
    Zondervan, 1985.

13. Morris, Charles and Eric. Christian Counselor as a Leader Vol.
    1. Puan Davao. Philbest, 1987.

14. Morrison, James. , ed. *Masterpieces of Religious Verses.* N.Y..
    Harper and Row Publication, 1817.

15. *Our Daily Bread Vol. 1.* Michigan . Discovery House Publisher,
    1993.

16. _________. *Vol. 2.* Michigan . Discovery House Publisher, 1995.

17. _________. Vol. 6 Michigan . Discovery House Publisher, 1997.

18. Pollit, R. and Wiltse, V. , *Helen Steiner Rice, Ambassador of
    Sunshine.* NY. Baker Book House, 1994.

19. Pritchard, Ray. *Man of Honor.* Wheaton, Ill. Crossway Books,
    1996.

20. Rice, Wayne. , *Hot Illustrations for Youth Talks,* El Cajon CA.
    Youth Specialties. 1994.

21. Sanders, Oswald. *Spiritual Leadership.* Chicago, Ill. Moody Press,
    1980.

22. Sala, Harold. *Winning Your Inner Struggles.* Manila. OMF
    Literature Inc. , 1988.

23. Sell, Charles and Virginia Sell. *Spiritual Intimacy for Couples.*
    Wheaton, Ill. Crossway Books, 1996.

24. *Seventh Day Adventist Bible Commentary 10 Volumes.*
Washington D.C. Review and Herald Publishing Association,
1978.

25. Tucker, James A. and Tucker, Priscilla. *Glimpse of God s Love.*
Washington D.C. Review and Herald Publishing Association,
1883.

26. White, Ellen G. *Acts of the Apostles.* Mountain View, CA. Pacific
Press Publishing Association. 1911.

27. __________. *Child Guidance.* Washington D.C. Review and
Herald Publishing Association, 1954.

28. __________. *Christ s Object Lessons.* Washington D.C. EGW
Publications, 1941.

29. __________. *Counsels to Parents and Teachers and Students.*
Washington D.C. EGW Publications, 1943.

30. __________. *Counsels to Stewardship.* Washington D.C. EGW
Publications, 1940.

31. __________. *Desire of Ages.* Mountain View, CA. Pacific Press
Publishing Association, 1940.

32. __________. *Education,* Mountain View, CA. Pacific Press
Publishing Association, 1952.

33. __________. *Evangelism.* Mountain View, CA. Pacific Press
Publishing Association, 1970.

34. __________, The *Faith I Live By.* Washington, D.C. Review and
Herald Publishing Association, 1973

35. _________, *God's Amazing Grace.* Washington, D.C. Review and Herald Publishing Association, 1973.

36. _________. *Gospel Workers.* Washington D.C. Review and Herald Publishing Association, 1948.

37. _________, *The Great Controversy Between Christ and Satan.* Mountain View, CA. Pacific Press Publishing Association. 1888.

38. _________. *Last Days Events.* Manila. Philippine Publishing House, 1999.

39. _________, *Lift Him Up.* Hagerstown, MD. Review and Herald Publishing Association, 1988.

40. _________, *Maranatha; The Lord Is Coming.* Washington, D.C. Review and Herald Publishing Association, 1976.

41. _________, *Medical Ministry.* Mountain View, CA. Pacific Press Publishing Association, 1963.

42. _________. *Messages to Young People.* Nashville, Tennessee. Southern Publishing Association, 1950.

43. _________. *Ministry of Healing.* Mountain View, CA. Pacific Press Publishing Association, 1942.

44. _________, *My Life Today.* Washington, D.C. Review and Herald Publishing Association, 1952.

45. _________, *Our High Calling.* Washington, D.C. Review and Herald Publishing Association, 1961

46. _________, *Pastoral Ministry.* Silver Spring, MD. General Conference Ministerial Association, 1995.

47. _________. *Patriarchs and Prophets.* Washington D.C. Review and Herald Publishing Association, 1958.

48. _________, *Reflecting Christ.* Hagerstown, MD. Review and Herald Publishing Association, 1985

49. _________. *Selected Messages Volume 2.* Washington D.C. Review and Herald Publishing Association, 1958.

50. _________. *Steps to Christ.* Phoenix, Arizona. Inspiration Books, 1971.

51. _________, *Sons and Daughters of God.* Washington, D.C. Review and Herald Publishing Association, 1955.

52. _________, *Spiritual Gifts.* 4 vols. Battle Creek, MI. Seventh.day Adventist Publishing Association, 1945.

53. _________. *Testimonies for the Church.* 9 vols. 1855.1909. Mountain View, CA. Pacific Press Publishing Association, 1948.

54. _________. *The Masters Immortal Sermons.* Mountain View, CA. Pacific Press Publishing Association, 1971.

55. _________, *The Seventh.day Adventist Bible Commentary.* Ellen G. White Comments. 7 vols. Washington, D.C. Review and Herald Publishing Association, 1970.

56. _________, *The Sanctified Life.* Washington, D.C. Review and Herald Publishing Association, 1956.

57. __________, *This Day With God.* Washington, D.C. Review and Herald Publishing Association, 1979.

58. __________, *Thoughts From the Mount of Blessing.* Mountain View, CA. Pacific Press Publishing Association, 1955.

59. __________, *The Upward Look.* Washington, D.C. Review and Herald Publishing Association, 1982.

60. __________, *The Review and Herald*

61. __________, *The Signs of the Times*

62. __________, Welfare Ministry. Washington, D.C. Review and Herald Publishing Association, 1952.

63. __________, *Ye Shall Receive Power.* Hagerstown, MD. Review and Herald Publishing Association, 1995.

64. *With God Nothing Is impossible.* New York. Bantam Books, 1988.

Other Books by
Marvin Marcelino

Path to Writing Spiritual Journal Volumes 1-8

101 Objects to Nurture Spirituality

Prepared for Life

SPEAK ENGLISH: Simple Progressive English Achievement Kit
Mastery of Vowels

SPEAK ENGLISH: Simple Progressive English Achievement Kit
Mastery of Consonants

One Anothering: A Biblical Guide to a Better Christian Interpersonal
Relations Volumes 1 & 2

Spiritual Interactive Learning Activities for the Youth

Spirituality versus Religiosity: What Works and What Saves

Take Off Thy Shoes: The Biblical Sanctuary Made Easy

Points of Argument: How to Detect Fallacy

I Am Wonderfully and Chemically Made

I Am Horribly and Chemically Fed

101 Sips of Life's Lessons

www.ingramcontent.com/pod-product-compliance
Lightning Source LLC
LaVergne TN
LVHW010513200726
843506LV00013B/2581